The Lines I Follow

*Walking the Spectrum of
Difference & Discovery*

ARNEL GAVIOLA

Copyright © 2025 by Arnel Gaviola.
Editors: Barclay Wilkinson
Monika Wilkinson
Graphic design: Arnel Gaviola
Content lay-out: Deborah Ngoho-Toling

Published by Untold Pilates

ISBN 978-1-0670138-2-0 (softcover)

ISBN 978-1-0670138-3-7 (ebook)

All rights reserved. No part of this book may be reproduced or transmitted in any form or by any means, electronic or mechanical, including photocopying, recording, or by any information storage and retrieval system without express written permission from the author, except in the case of brief quotations embodied in critical reviews and certain other noncommercial uses permitted by copyright law.

Printed in the United States of America.

Dedication

To anyone who has ever felt lost in their own mind.

The world is fast paced and chaotic, and increasingly so with modern technology. Arnel generously shares his internal world offering insight into understanding how life on the spectrum has shaped his way of being and in doing so, crafts a story that inspires curiosity about the taken for granted world we interact with everyday.

Dr Thea Wass (DClinPsy)

Acknowledgements

To my family, thank you for being there through every thought, every sentence, and every curious observation.

To Barclay and Monika, friends and editors, thank you for your guidance and support along the way.

To my mind, thank you for helping me pursue this project.

About the Author

My name is Arnel Gaviola. I live full-time in my van, where the road and horizon keep giving me new shapes, stories, and reflections. Living on the autism spectrum, I see the world through lines, whether in rain, wind, buildings, or people. I run my own Pilates studio, paint, love animals, and find meaning in creating quietly and intentionally.

Much of my writing comes from the stillness of van life, where time slows down and small details reveal their hidden rhythms. This book grew from my reflections on the mind, perception, and the search for understanding between consciousness and the physical world. With my best friend Alba, I keep moving forward with curiosity and heart, hoping to show others the beauty hidden within everyday patterns.

Contents

Life in My Tiny Home on Wheels 1

- How my van operates as a personal sensory room:...............11

Everyday Lines 15

- How I process stories and why I ask questions:....................34
- How I perceive eyes and glancing patterns in conversations:..36

Misaligned 51

- How my anxiety develops in stages:.......................................68
- Why I prefer physical interaction in relationships:...............75

Reading the World 79

- How my hyper-observation functions in everyday situations: 90

Reflection and Insight 93

- On Campervan 94
- Off Medication 95
- On Painting 97
- On Music...99
- On Sounds 100
- On Technology..102
- On Animals...104
- On Mountains 106
- On Beaches 108
- On Questions..109
- On Hyper-Focus 111

- The Foam Universe Equation..113
- Awareness Gravity Theory:
  How Consciousness Shapes the Pull of Reality................117
- On Stimming..120
- On Community...122
- On Masking..125
- On Money..127
- Final Reflections...129

Introduction

I want this book to be as grounded and authentic as possible. I'm not a professional writer or a novelist—far from it. I'm not an academic achiever, and I don't have formal training in storytelling. English isn't even my first language; in fact, it's the part I struggle with the most. Still, I hope to show that I can carry my story without needing academic credentials. Through this creative work, I want to share my journey and encourage others. My aim is to show that having autism spectrum disorder (ASD) and fewer qualifications are not barriers when curiosity, creativity, and imagination lead the way.

This book is a personal account of my life through the lens of someone recently diagnosed with ASD. It's a story of exploration, observation, and how I navigate the narrow spaces of my world. I hope it offers insight to mental health professionals, parents of autistic children, and anyone walking a similar path. My aim is to share how a mind like mine experiences the world—noticing details most people overlook and living in ways that feel both ordinary and profoundly different.

I also want to acknowledge that this is my second book. The most challenging part of my first one wasn't the writing, composition, or layout. It was the photo shoot, which proved physically demanding. We worked for four hours straight without a single break, using only a phone camera. In the end, it wasn't skill or resources that carried me through, but determination and persistence.

I also feel more confident now compared to when I wrote my first book. I believe creativity has no boundaries if you commit to it. Why do I say that? My first big project outside my professional field was stripping and painting an entire vintage car—a full restoration. From buying an air compressor to figuring out the smallest tools, I took everything apart with just YouTube as my guide.

Next came converting my tiny car into a home, and later my campervan: a pull-out bed with storage, overhead shelves, side compartments, and new flooring. My latest project was building three Pilates reformers in my garage for my studio. I taught myself everything, from handling a drill to using a sewing machine for upholstery. I'm not a builder, carpenter, furniture designer, mechanic, or panel beater, but every project was completed through nothing more than creativity, curiosity, and commitment. These experiences are exactly why I've approached this book the way I have.

Some readers might feel that a few points in this book could be summed up in a single word or explained by science. Perhaps. But this book isn't about proving anything—it's about the journey, reflection, and insights found in the lines I follow.

I hope this reaches you with the same sense of value and curiosity, allowing you to walk in my world.

Life in My Tiny Home on Wheels

You might wonder why I've titled this chapter this way. Am I just going to talk about living in a van? Not exactly. My tiny home on wheels is where my story revolves; it's where I discovered senses and observations I had never noticed before and helped me identify things about myself and the world that had previously gone unnoticed.

It all started with a simple preference for a vehicle. The first car I ever owned was a small hatchback, what some might call a "grandma car," followed by an SUV, which I even equipped with a small picnic table. I supplied it with containers filled with food, water, and essentials—little experiments in self-sufficiency. Later, I returned to a smaller hatchback with a collapsible back seat, complete with a pillow and blanket, so I could take a short nap during work breaks. I had no idea that one day I would be living in a van, but in hindsight, I think it was already a sign. Life's direction shifted, and I forgot about these small experiments. Years later, when I decided to take it to the next level, I had another small car, and that's when I began exploring micro tiny homes online—YouTube, Google, anything I could find.

For nearly four months, I spent almost every free moment imagining the possibilities, planning how I could transform a small space into a functional home. When I finally felt ready to build it from scratch, I started with a cardboard prototype—a single foldable bed and a small kitchen sink beside it at the back of my car—just to see how it might look. It took me some time to move from cardboard to structural plywood because I needed a few tools. My hands weren't made for handling tools, and I also didn't know much about using them either. Still, I was focused and determined.

Once it was finished, I spent my first night right outside my house. Then one day, my flatmate asked if I wanted to join them for a two-night weekend at a holiday park. It was the perfect opportunity to test my micro home and see if I truly loved it or if it was just born out of boredom. At the campsite, we were greeted by crowds of people, kids on skateboards and scooters, and cars towing fishing boats—a chaotic scene that sharply contrasted with the solitude I experienced that night. The desire for hidden privacy, like being inside a time capsule, somehow ignited my imagination. That weekend helped me make a clear decision.

After two months of scouring the marketplace, I finally owned my first-ever campervan. At first, I was both scared and excited, filled with questions, uncertainties, and situations I had never faced. But after three months, I settled in and told myself: I will never go back to living in a house again. That was the moment everything began. For the first time in my life, I spent long stretches of time alone, in isolation, surrounded by nature, listening to the wind, birds, rain, and ocean. It felt like the perfect space to explore myself, to truly see and understand who I was. After a year of living in it, I noticed that I became more attuned to subtleties; and I began seeing rain differently.

> "I began to imagine each raindrop landing on the roof had a shape, like a thousand chopsticks breaking into pieces like uncooked rice, bouncing in chaos and covering every inch of my van's surface."

At first, I let it pass, thinking my mind was just adjusting to this new lifestyle. Maybe this was simply what happens when spending too much time alone. Over time, though, it became normalized. And since it was winter, with constant rains and wind, there was nothing else to do but experience this new perspective. Yet the more I tried to ignore it, the more insistently it demanded my attention. The raindrops hitting the window beside my bed became visual, each one taking on its own shape and impossible to ignore, especially when there was nothing else to see or hear. All I saw were those

> "Single drops, carrying a mixture of lines, highlights, and shadows, crystal clear like a baby's tear."

I had no choice but to notice, especially when I was driving, watching thousands of drops burst across the windshield like fireworks, almost like choreography. It always began with a few tiny drops, followed by medium ones, then large droplets—a sequence that would repeat with every pass of the wiper.

This new but random sense of boredom, as I called it, began to escalate. Ordinary ripples spreading from a single raindrop hitting puddles outside now revealed distinct lines. At one point, I even crawled under my stove to check if the gas was leaking, worried I might be poisoned or hallucinating. But it was sealed tight. I thought about sharing this experience with my close friends, but at the back of my mind, I feared they might think it was nonsense—the same nonsense I sometimes believed myself—a waste of their time. So I moved on. I just closed my curtains whenever it rained and tried to ignore it. After all, no matter how I looked at it, it was still the same rain I had seen a million times and the same puddles of water. And again, I thought to myself:

> "As long as it doesn't affect my daily routines, then why bother?"

Moving forward, carrying this new wave of experience, driving on familiar roads began to feel different. It became a mixture of real and illusion,

> "My van moving forward, and then, in the blink of an eye, feeling as if the van was stationary while the road moved toward me."

It was like those car racing simulators. I remember thinking, "Wow! What a new way to see it!" And because it didn't happen all the time, it felt even more puzzling. From then on, it just kept building. Everything I saw on the road—cars, trucks, bikes, scooters, boats, trees, road signs, tires, advertisements, beams of headlights—and even the tiniest details like the design of a door handle, the shape of a gas tank cover, the pattern of a tail light, the curve of a bumper, the hooks for towing, or the outline of a window

> "Carried lines and angles that became dominant. Those shapes and edges stood out more than anything else. All of it stacked in my head for a few seconds before fading."

It was overwhelming at times, yet strangely natural, because I had been aware of the road and its details for as long as I could remember. Maybe my mind has always worked this way, or maybe it was the result of isolation.

> "Sometimes I even think there are two sides of the brain: one managing the real-time event, and the other quietly observing it."

I don't really know how the mind works in general, I've never studied it at all. I can only rely on what my own mind tells me and what it allows me to notice. That's how I've noticed my thoughts have patterns too. I don't just see patterns emerging in the outside world, I see them within myself too.

If there's such a thing as selective memory, then I think there's also selective patterning. Not everything I look at shows a pattern, and I don't catch every dominant line that shapes things either. Instead, my attention zooms in on particular patterns, like a lens picking out certain threads while the rest stay blurred.

Pattern recognition has proven to be very important for understanding the world's mechanics. It supports us and provides answers to questions like mine. But at this stage of my life, I've also become fascinated by how my mind tries to venture out of its usual paths, just to find comfortable answers that satisfy me.

Let's go back to my outside world. When I'm not driving and it's not raining, I usually stay in my van, parked somewhere quiet—on the beach or in an empty car park—either sleeping, cooking, eating, browsing, cleaning, or just lying down. It gives me time to observe and feel the weather: the warmth of the sun, the gentle breeze. I watch families with kids playing, people having picnics, and those who are active—joggers, bikers, and walkers—along with dogs and seagulls moving through the space.

When I watch them rise and fall through the wide open space, their movements feel too deliberate to be random.

"Do air pockets matter to them? Convenience? The time of day?"

I even joke that such details would only matter if the birds were carrying human passengers. Still, I find myself wondering:

> *"Do these birds have free will? And if they do, are they even aware of it? Because if not, then what's the purpose of having it?"*

From above, I'm sure everything they see below could serve ase a landing strip, yet they always choose a very specific spot. When they land on my roof, I can hear the sharp sound of their claws—a sound once meaningless now forming a tempo or pattern in my mind. I know it exists only in my imagination, yet I can't help but wonder:

> *"How can we ever be sure what we hear or see is truly real if no one else is there to confirm it? How do you prove to your own mind that what you experience is truthful?"*

I know birds have an intricate internal compass, but what puzzles me most is the specific direction and exact path they choose, as if they own every inch of the sky.

> *"I sometimes think of birds as the physical reflection of our skies."*

Everything feels alive, patterned, almost like a program,

> "The chaos that somehow feels organized, similar to the rain. The significance of lines that shape everyone and everything in front of me becomes clear, just as what I observed on the road or in the park."

The way people turn their heads, how they move along paths, how children do the same when running, and how someone stumbles and falls—all of this I see within an invisible order. Perhaps it's because I don't know what they're thinking or planning, or perhaps my heightened attention has sharpened my observation and changed my perspective.

As I sat there calmly, watching my observations fade and taking a deep breath, I thought about how I wished life were really a program, where choice no longer mattered, where goals weren't a struggle, where direction needed no planning. A life where anger, pain, love, happiness, and every emotion were simply expressions of being. A life considered fair, with nothing and no one left to blame.

I've probably heard people say, "You just need someone to talk to." Maybe that works if the person shares my curiosity and asks the same kind of questions. But if not, the conversation just becomes something to wrap up quickly—and that's always the case.

"So is keeping it to myself better? Well, it doesn't matter."

These questions usually fade after running around in my head for a while, unless something distracts me first. They get tangled up with a different question, then another, until they all blur together. It's like trying to catch smoke with your hands: the more I try to hold onto one thought, the more it slips into the next, until finally it all just drifts away.

How my van operates as a personal sensory room:

1. Controlled environment
   I can adjust what I see, hear, and feel, creating a predictable and safe space. I control how much light comes in or switch to my calm interior lights when I need a softer atmosphere.

2. Heightened sensory awareness

   Sounds, like raindrops on the roof, feel amplified and vivid, letting me notice details I might otherwise miss. When I need quiet, I can close the curtains to soften or block the sound.

3. Solitude and focus

   Being able to move freely, find a comfortable spot, and choose solitude lets me think, reflect, and recharge without distraction.

4. Self-regulation

   It's my familiar space where I can calm myself and process intense emotions. It helps me reset when I'm overloaded, leaving me feeling refreshed, much like a sensory room in therapy.

"Does our brain comprehend better when lines are used as a tool for learning to play musical instruments?"

Everyday Lines

Some might think I have a calm lifestyle because I don't have fixed weekly responsibilities like rent, a mortgage, or electric bills. But there's also a trade-off. I move around a lot because self-contained carparks have limited stays per month. To avoid too much movement, I need to plan ahead and find somewhere to stay for the night that's close to work. During summer, with so many tourists in campervans, even careful planning doesn't always work because places get taken, which can be a bit stressful.

The most important part is hoping I'm not in an open car park, because there might be kids blasting music at 2 a.m. There's nothing you can do—it's a public space, and you definitely don't want to confront them about the volume, especially if they might be drunk. I also understand them, because I was like that when I was younger.

I still listen to my favorite music, but more maturely now—music that's peaceful to my ears and doesn't need to be blasted at high volume from a sick stereo setup. Speaking of which, I have a basic one with a monitor for my reverse camera, although I'm a bit particular about the quality so I can hear each instrument in any song. Maybe it's from being trained on piano, guitar, violin, and saxophone. Yes, I took lessons out of my love for music, and I even played in a band. The last one was as a bassist in a worship ministry.

The frustrating part of learning to play an instrument is learning how to read notes. In the past, looking at notes never bothered me. But lately, while learning the saxophone, I've had a curious question:

> "Why do we use lines to translate and understand sounds?"

> "Does our brain comprehend better when lines are used as a tool for learning to play musical instruments?"

Looking at music notes that all look identical, arranged side by side or above and below on horizontal bars—how is that supposed to be easy?

Maybe some people eventually find it natural, but it feels like I'm forced to use a method that doesn't work for me.

> "Every time I look at music notes, they remind me of my own fingers. The lines look like the fingers themselves, while the roundness of the notes reminds me of fingertips."

I used to think that the musical notes sitting on each line were the exact representation of my violin strings—all I had to do was press the string that matched the note's position. I'm not sure if that made things easier or even more confusing. Everything about it seemed to involve lines: the notes drawn on lines, the strings arranged in lines, even the bow that had to move in a straight line. It was too much for me to process, and I never reached a point where I felt good at it.

With the guitar and bass, it was simpler because I read chords instead of notes. The saxophone wasn't confusing at all—my fingers didn't move too much as I didn't need to look, just feel. I was pressing soft circular buttons instead of strings.

Then comes the hardest part of learning a musical instrument for me: being in tune. I remember my saxophone teacher saying it's all about the connection between my teeth, lips, and air, combined with practice. But how can my brain recognize my teacher's tone as "perfect" while my own tone sounds different? Two different tones, yet my brain somehow insists that mine is correct too. If my brain already knows what the "right" tone should sound like, why does it tell me that what I produce matches that perfect pitch? It feels like my brain has a double standard, especially when you're still new to music. Like when two people sing the same note and both believe they're perfect, yet only one hit it correctly.

If we return to my observations in the park and zoom in on animals in relation to sound, I notice something peculiar: seagulls share an identical cry, sparrows a nearly indistinguishable chirp. Even nature itself—wind, waves, thunder, lightning—speaks with a kind of sameness, yet dogs and humans don't. Maybe those birds do sound different, but my ears aren't trained to catch the subtle differences. Yet if it's simply a matter of training, how come I can still hear the differences in voices from people in a country I've never been exposed to?

A flock of sparrows in the morning blends into one unified chorus, while a group of foreigners passing by never sound the same. Science says our voices are learned for complex communication, while birds' calls are mostly fixed for survival. If that's true, why doesn't the pattern hold across all species? Parrots, for example, can mimic complex language. Dogs don't use complex communication like humans, yet within the same breed, their voices aren't identical. At this, I wonder:

> "Why are most sounds in the world so stable, while ours remain endlessly varied?"

How about communication, whether written or verbal? Similar to music, writing consists of lines, and verbal communication involves sounds. The difference is that the lines in writing don't need to be perfectly precise across the horizontal guides on paper, they can even exist without any grid. Likewise, the sounds we produce verbally don't need to be perfect pitch either: they just need to convey meaning.

The standards for writing are far less strict than those of musical notation, where even a small mistake can distort the meaning. Yet writing holds a far greater weight: it is the window through which we unlock the keys to every dimension of education. Without writing, learning cannot progress beyond fleeting sounds or memory. But this raises a similar question:

> "Does our mind comprehend better when lines are used to learn written language?"

From art to science, from calculation to literature, lines seem to be the thread weaving intellect itself.

> "Did our mind give us a hint to use lines to maximize its potential to learn, remember, create? Did it require the order of lines? Or did lines emerge as our own invention, a reflection of the brain's hidden architecture?"

And if it did give us a hint,

> "Is it conscious or unconscious? Could it be that our mind already carries some kind of system with something built-in that suggests lines might be a fundamental way our mind organizes learning?"

To me, it feels less like our consciousness learns about lines and more like it already knows them, even before we do.

And if we talk about the educational system, particularly my school, all of us kids—girls and boys alike—were taught the same way in class. The exercises, the exact paper to use, the specific pen or pencil, even the kind of eraser were all listed as requirements for our parents to buy. Then came the hours, days, and years mastering each stroke. Yet the results were never the same. Each person developed their own interpretation.

> "But how does our mind manage to create its own style while still learning the mechanics of writing?"

For me, it feels as if interpretation can only happen when there is some prior experience, or when the brain carries a hidden knowledge, quietly guiding each of us toward our own expression. It's the same way I was given the ability to sketch, draw, and paint at an early age, long before I even knew such skills existed.

I remember reading news a while back about a few people who, after head trauma, suddenly acquired knowledge they didn't possess before. One was an American man who became a math genius, a phenomenon called "acquired savant syndrome," and another was a Dutch teenager who developed the ability to speak a foreign language after knee surgery, sometimes referred to as "foreign language syndrome."

> "Could this be a good example of how we all carry hidden knowledge, quietly waiting to be discovered?"

Or maybe our muscles play a role in how our penmanship differs.

> "But if they do, which muscles are responsible?"

I don't remember anyone mentioning anything about hand muscles when I was learning how to write or paint—which muscles were responsible for which movements, or what stretches we should do. The only thing

I ever learned from it was that the more hours you practiced, the better your handwriting became. But no one ever explained why, or what the hand was actually learning. And if we were all trained with the same writing method, developing the same muscle groups,

"Then why can't we all produce similar results?"

Even though my siblings and I ate, slept, and studied in the same place, our handwriting still turned out different, as if each hand had its own way of thinking. Perhaps that's why each of us develops our own handwriting style, or our own way of interpreting perfect pitch, because this built-in knowledge already exists, quietly waiting to be expressed. Maybe what we call talent is simply that built-in knowledge revealing itself in the physical world.

If the mind can guide our complex hands to write, how much more can it guide our bodies in movement? I've been working with movement for 24 years as a Pilates instructor, and it never ceases to amaze me. I still have questions from time to time, but the answers seem to reveal themselves through observation, practice, and experience. And because I don't read much and don't know where to begin, my questions often feel like the old chicken-or-egg riddle. For example, if we came from fish,

> *"Did their bodies grow fins first without joints, like simple extensions? Or did the joints appear right away, already prepared for movement, waiting for us to discover how to use them?"*

or

> *"Did we start out sitting down, closer to the ground, and then gradually develop knees through evolution? Or did someone suddenly appear with knees and later learn to bend them, realizing that having knees feels so much better?"*

I know science has already explained how fish develop. It makes sense on paper, but to me, it still feels like a theory without a clear physical trail to follow. I mean,

> "Did our tiny fish-mind really 'decide' to lengthen its fins one day simply because consciousness wanted to wander on land?"

And once they were long enough,

> "Did our consciousness bend them at the right angle?"

I can't imagine a fish-like creature having a mind capable of designing something so complex. The fossils we have now are only fragments, pieces of a bigger picture still missing. Even the story of humans standing upright feels unfinished. Drawings of our ancestors, bent over to fully upright, are just illustrations. They make me wonder:

> "Why would anyone choose to stand when crawling on all fours is faster, more agile and stable, and, in some ways, safer?"

I imagine those early moments…

> "Did our crawling cousins look at the first upright walkers and laugh at their awkwardness? Or did the standing ones laugh back, seeing something the others couldn't?"

Science says standing gives us an advantage—to spot predators from afar. But to me, standing itself could make us more visible to other predators as well. In my small world, standing doesn't seem like the smartest option. It feels like trading stability for vulnerability. Much like designing a four-passenger car balanced on just two wheels.

> *"Why would nature ask us to balance everything on only two legs?"*

Just like in Chapter 1, I've observed toddlers falling repeatedly, spending countless hours learning to stabilize themselves from an unstable position. Most of our movement is fundamentally about stabilizing the body to maintain an upright, aligned posture. That's why we swing our arms opposite to our legs—it improves efficiency and helps maintain balance while walking. Try moving your arms and legs on the same side in the same direction and you'll immediately feel how awkward and unstable it is.

Freeing our hands to use tools also doesn't necessarily require standing; we can still use our hands while sitting.

> *"Could it be that our crawling ancestors imitated a standing tree by rising upright, gaining that advantage without having to rely on the tree itself?"*

This is also why individuals with exceptional balance, such as circus performers or dancers, are so remarkable. Their skill shows what becomes possible when the body learns to push beyond the natural limits of upright posture. Yet the hours they devote to training are constant; the moment practice stops, the body slowly returns to its baseline pattern.

It's similar to what I noticed with toddlers learning to walk: they seem to start off a little misaligned, crawling and stumbling, gradually figuring out how to stand upright. Over time, they find that invisible line of balance, learning to hold themselves steady. Later in life, it almost feels as if the body drifts back toward that original state, as if reminding us of how we began. There's just too much mystery in the world waiting to be answered.

> *"It would be nice and convenient if we could simply reach into our minds and pull out any answer we need."*

But I guess society needs a shared truth to stay aligned in one understanding.

To study movement is to study endlessly in order to notice how every small feedback travels through the body and outward. And when you do, you can't help but see how the body is built. Look closer, starting from the larger sections and narrowing in, and you'll find bones, muscles, and tissues stacked together, all aligned along horizontal and vertical planes. The lines give shape; the alignment gives foundation and function.

And if we're talking about body shape, when did it start to become so significant and important? Is it because a better shape is seen as a reflection of good health? But we know that being healthy doesn't necessarily show in one's shape. I just can't understand when body shape became, in a way, a victim of sexuality.

It's not just structure; even feeling itself seems to move along lines.

> "Sometimes I wonder why sensations, whether from touching or licking, feel like they're traced by lines."

Is it because our sensory neurons are arranged in lines? Even something as intimate as sexual intercourse seems to follow lines.

And if we talk about touch, each one of us has a different take on it. Some are touchy and some are not. Some talk with hands in their pockets, while others move their hands like a maestro conducting an orchestra. Some of us barely react when touched, while others are sensitive. I don't mind being tapped on the shoulder by a stranger, but that person must give me some warning so I'm not startled.

Otherwise, a lot of questions would jolt through my head:

> "Why did they do that?"
>
> "Are they trying to get my attention? And for what?"

These questions will loop in my head while we are in a conversation, and my focus will be affected. And if it's not explained afterward, I tend to assume a lot of things, taking my social cues in the wrong direction.

> *"Are these reactions normal?"*

If you ask me if I'm touchy: not really. And when it comes to intimacy, I'm more deliberate, guided by plans rather than feelings. I just feel more comfortable and safer if I do it that way.

> *"Even random shoulder-to-shoulder contact while walking with friends can create a whole whirlwind in my mind to wonder about."*

It's like my brain is wired to snap—once the barrier is crossed, chaos spills out.

It reminds me how much detail my brain randomly picks up. It's the same thing I notice when I'm at the park, just closer and more personal. From the fine strands of hair and how they fall along the scalp, to how the eyebrows, eyes, nose, mouth, and ears sit in quiet symmetry. I also think our expressions are all carried by lines—the curve of a smile, the narrowing of the eyes, whatever we feel is shaped by them. And when I get the chance to observe people more deeply, I see even more—lines that seem to carry stories about life itself.

Often, when people pass by me while climbing a mountain, I can clearly notice the details of their complexion: from the smooth, powdery texture of youthful skin to the flakier texture of more mature skin. The natural signs of aging, each one with its own mark, are like fingerprints or ridges on our feet.

I think we often define wrinkles only in terms of our physical bodies: the composition of skin or how it interacts with the environment. But for me, they mean something deeper. Wrinkles are more than skin and environment; they are the imprint of experience, translated into conscious information over time. Somehow, these condensed feelings, stored in the parts of our brain we use over the years, are projected outward, and that projection is what we call wrinkles. I imagine each wrinkle as a stratum of rock compressed through time, a visible record of the experiences that shaped us.

This idea of lines continues beyond wrinkles. Even the way we describe faces—hairline, jawline—it's all lines. And if you look closer inside the body, from muscles and tendons to organs and veins, everything still follows some kind of line. Even DNA, drawn in books, is shown through lines. I don't know why, but somehow, lines keep showing up in this journey.

And as we move lower, we can see the slope of the collarbones to the placement of the shoulders. And from these observations, I usually come back to a similar question about evolution. If we call ourselves a product of intelligent design, then:

> "Why is our hair scattered in patches across our bodies? Why do we need hats and clothes to protect ourselves from the environment we evolved into? Why do we need eye protection and still never fully get used to the sun's glare? Why did we evolve by losing our sharper teeth,

> "capable of tearing meat, and instead rely on knives? Why did we evolve by giving up so much?"

> "If we're really meant for this Earth, how does all of this even make sense?"

Imagine a tank filled with the best technology possible, built to withstand the enemy's capabilities, then taking away its metal shell and sending it to war completely exposed. Now compare that to our prehistoric cousins, whose bodies were perfectly designed to endure everything, and then imagine stripping away those parts that made them strong, leaving their weaknesses exposed. It doesn't make sense.

> "Should making our minds stronger make the rest of our bodies weaker? Why must other parts be sacrificed for the evolution of the brain?"

It feels like a selfish act of our minds, leaving everything else behind. And now we have to exercise, train, and push our bodies to be fit and strong, just to reverse the mistakes of our minds. You might ask,

> *"Aren't you tired of hearing these questions in your head? And why not just Google them?"*

As a child, I remember my family always reminding me to keep my mouth shut whenever we watched movies at home or in the cinema. I had a habit of asking a billion questions while the film was playing. Perhaps that was already one of the signs I overlooked, because I assumed I was just a curious kid like every other child.

How I process stories and why I ask questions:

1. Struggles with gaps in the narrative
   - When an event or explanation is missing, I can't automatically fill in the blanks. This applies not only to movies, but also to documentaries—for example, about evolution or history—where important details are assumed or skipped.
   - Jump cuts or unexplained events feel incomplete or confusing.

2. Need for logical continuity

    My mind replays key moments, trying to connect them and make sense of the overall story.

3. Use questions as a processing tool
    - Asking questions aloud or to myself helps me map information into a coherent structure. This is especially when there are complex plots or events that occur simultaneously and ambiguous or skipped-over scenes.
    - It's not always about getting an answer—sometimes it's just about seeing the whole picture.

In one of my sessions, my psychologist told me that a common trait of ASD is difficulty making eye contact and reading what the eyes express, or picking up on social cues. I had never really noticed it before, until I took an ASD-specific eye test and discovered that I struggled with it.

How I perceive eyes and glancing patterns in conversations:

1. Physical shape of the eyes

   A larger or slightly rounded shape often gives me a quiet sense of intimidation, as if the person's gaze holds more weight or intensity than I can manage.

2. Pupil dilation or contraction

   When pupils expand or shrink, it makes me feel exposed—as though they're scanning deeper into me than I'm prepared to show.

3. Eye movement and focus
   - Quick, rigid, or deliberate movements—almost like the careful, stiff walk of a small bird—make me feel as if I'm being studied just as closely in return.
   - A blank, prolonged stare causes my mind to question itself.

4. Emotional effects
   - These small visual details bring emotional discomfort I can't easily ignore.

- They make me feel uneasy, as if I'm intruding on someone's privacy.
- They make me feel vulnerable and unsure of how to respond.

I used to think this was just part of my insecurities, not part of my ASD. Normally, when someone feels threatened, their reaction might automatically block certain thoughts, maybe including the ability to pick up social cues. But even when I stare straight at someone, I've realized I still don't really have a clue. Only when it's obvious—if someone is laughing, crying, or telling me they're upset—do I understand. I never truly knew how important social cues were until I became aware of them. And then I ask:

> "Where does my mind get that sense of discomfort just from looking at someone's eyes? If it can pick up that kind of feedback, does that mean I can read social cues but simply read them incorrectly? Does having ASD mean that social cues are distorted?"

Then, more questions follow:

> "Does a lack of social cues mean something is missing within me, or is there something blocking them, causing that absence?"

And maybe because I felt uncomfortable looking at them, my brain seemed to rely on hearing instead, trying to determine whether they were comfortable with me. Perhaps this is why I often interpret things literally, attending only to what people actually say.

Then you might ask:

> "How did I survive or avoid making eye contact, especially as a Pilates teacher, when every day people are trying to engage with me?"

Before I explain, I think this question needs a bit of backstory. I didn't just avoid eye contact; I avoided being the center of attention, especially in serious or formal settings. It didn't really affect me if it was something fun, like being the spotlight in a group joke, performing in front of an audience when I was in a band, or even being a movie extra. But if a teacher called on me to answer a question, give a report in front of the class, or just introduce myself, or respond to a roll call, that was a real struggle. I can't count how many times I skipped class for that reason.

All I could think during those moments was that I was a very insecure person. But now, I think it has more to do with my autism.

Even after all these years of teaching, I still haven't gotten used to the discomfort of being watched. Over time, I've developed ways to blend in. That's why I'm very particular about the studio equipment arrangement. I need to see if I can move freely, not just for teaching purposes, but also to avoid having their eyes on me. I don't know if my clients notice, but,

> "I usually go in the opposite direction from wherever they're facing."

That's how I camouflage and blend into the studio without affecting my teaching.

> "The only situation where I feel cornered and completely uncomfortable is when I'm having a session with my counsellor or psychologist. It's ironic, really—the very place where I'm supposed to get help is where I feel the most uneasy."

Over the years, I've been able to develop my own way of navigating social situations in class, which somehow echoes my experience growing up with five siblings and all of us developing different preferences.

I grew up in a great family, and I was the second youngest, which I think made me the second favourite and closest to my mom. In a big family like ours, every meal time meant there was a lot of food on the table for everyone to share. No one had a special plate or a different diet. Despite that, each of us had our own tastes. One sibling preferred this, another leaned toward that. Somehow, even though we ate the same meals, our individual preferences slowly emerged over time.

That made me wonder:

> "If we were all raised by the same parents, in the same house, eating the same food, how did we end up so different? It's the same observation I made about handwriting—how, even under the same conditions, each of us develops in our own unique way."

But those differences never carried a negative weight. Maybe because they never turned into fights or conflicts. Instead, they just felt like part of who we were becoming, part of growing up, part of life, I guess.

> "It amazes me how each of our consciousnesses seems to follow its own alignment. No matter how many traditions, rules, or cultural expectations exist, the mind often finds its own path, especially when it feels safe and comfortable."

Back then, any food served was simply meant to be eaten; it had nothing to do with diets or health plans. I knew nothing about "healthy eating." I only knew how food looked, smelled, and tasted. It wasn't until after university, when I began living a more active lifestyle, that I started paying attention to how what I ate affected my body and mind.

> "Over time, my preferences began to shift, guided no longer solely by my inner thoughts, but by intention, purpose, and the outcomes I wanted to achieve."

Over the years, I went from eating anything without thinking to tracking calories, and eventually, becoming a vegetarian—quite a turnaround. It happened more by circumstance. Meat and seafood became little more than daydreams, while chickpeas, lentils, vegetable-based meat alternatives, and pastries filled my plate.

Then, just recently, I noticed something curious: the way I ate seemed to follow a pattern. I'd often start from left to right, or from the top of my plate downward, as if there were an invisible order guiding every bite.

> "Eating felt more satisfying when I followed a sequence, as if the food needed to be organized before it could be truly enjoyed."

Or maybe it's simply the "right" way to eat, an unspoken form of etiquette I was never formally taught. Perhaps I learned it by observing others, or maybe our evolving brains are naturally wired to follow that pattern, to find comfort in the order of movement without even realizing it.

It struck me that this sense of order exists everywhere, not just at the table. Even in cooking competitions on TV programs, food isn't simply made to taste good—it's arranged with precision, each element aligned for presentation. It's as if the arrangement itself is an extension of how the dish will taste. The way chefs slice, plate, and even lift food to their mouths seem to follow straight lines. And when we eat, I've noticed how rarely anyone chews in circles. From licking ice cream to biting something on a stick, our movements almost always follow a direct path.

Even within us, the same order continues. The teeth line up in rows, the tongue forms ridges, and the throat shapes a passage. It makes me wonder:

> "Are they arranged to guide the process of chewing so that our lined-up digestive system can break food down into nutrition more efficiently?"

If one of the purposes of our brain's evolution is curiosity,

> "Why can't it avoid complications? Why would it resort to seemingly illogical ways of preparing food if its sole purpose is to fuel us and keep us functioning?"

Because once food enters our mouths, all the intricate work of cooking disappears. A boiled egg, perfectly simple, reminds me of that—no decoration, no lining, no fuss, yet it fulfills its purpose just the same.

Have you ever noticed that there's never a single image of an obese caveman in all our science books, nor any story of Jesus healing someone from obesity? It makes me think,

> "Somewhere along the way, our collective consciousness chose complexity over logic."

or

> "Our consciousness no longer cares for the development of the body; it acts out of selfishness, prioritising knowledge born from curiosity."

We began preparing food in ways that disconnected us from its true purpose.

Today, we have the knowledge, the tools, the technology to create food that keeps us well—yet we look around and see the opposite happening.

Meanwhile, those we call "primitive" lived without diet plans or supplements, yet no one seemed burdened by excess. Not all of them were hunters chasing wild rabbits; I'm sure there were artists, cooks, and thinkers too. Still, history never told us they were obese.

I understand that food doesn't only sustain the body; it also influences the mind in subtle ways, shaped by experience. For instance, whenever I drink cola, it feels harmless at first, but after months of drinking it regularly, my anxiety begins to rise.

The following story shows exactly what I mean about the quiet ways food can trigger responses in both body and mind.

There was a time when I ate mostly meat, until my partner at the time expressed her concerns and warned me that it was no longer healthy—that I could die if I continued. From that instant, something triggered within me.

> "I stood up from the dining table, clutching my neck as my airway suddenly tightened and I couldn't breathe. My vision narrowed, sounds faded, and my thoughts began to spin—another anxiety attack. I leaned against the wall and slowly slid down to the floor, waiting for the tension to loosen just enough for the tears to come."

It wasn't just the physical feeling that unsettled me, but also the overwhelming confusion—it was the first time it had ever happened. I couldn't believe how much the power of suggestion could influence both my mind and body. After that, I became more mindful about how often and what kind of food I ate. Even though I'm a vegetarian now, I adjust my menu every few months. For example, I might rotate between lentils, chickpeas, broccoli, mushrooms, and rice, then later switch the rice for noodles.

Then you might ask: do I get bored eating the same or similar food?

> "I usually stick to what I think brings peace to my mind—not just with food, but also with the clothes I wear, the colors I like, the places I visit, and the people I spend time with. The more peaceful it is, the

> more comfortable I feel, helping me keep anxiety at bay. Maybe that's what they mean when they say that ASD often comes with repetitive behaviors."

Sometimes, I think of anxiety as the scientific word for chaos. This leads me to my next question:

> "Why does my mind choose chaos instead of peace when my coping mechanisms fail?"

And if we talk about chaos, I often think of a tree, its branches growing in every direction, its leaves scattered without order. Yet somehow, that chaos forms a shape we find beautiful. Especially when I think that the tree's disorder serves a purpose: it gives shade, oxygen, and even symbolizes peace. So then I wonder:

> "If the human mind is more intelligent than any tree, why does its own form of chaos often feel unbearable? Why does our inner disorder rarely turn into something as gentle or meaningful as a tree's?"

Finally, when I think more deeply about evolution, in my own limited understanding, I begin to see curiosity as one of its defining traits. If curiosity is part of evolution, then evolution has designed our minds to explore the unknown. But if the unknown exists to be discovered, then it means our minds are willing to take the risk of uncertainty. So my question is:

> *"Do you think our consciousness knows that uncertainty can cause stress, depression, and anxiety?"*

And has our consciousness already somewhat known the future—that stress, depression, and anxiety are just small sacrifices for what it will gain? Because if it doesn't know, I'm sure we'd still be sitting in our caves, looking at each other, wondering what's for dinner tomorrow. Sometimes I wonder why our mind chooses to wander into the wilderness when everything else in nature seems content in its stable conditions.

> *"And at what point in our primitive past did we begin to trade stability for uncertainty?"*

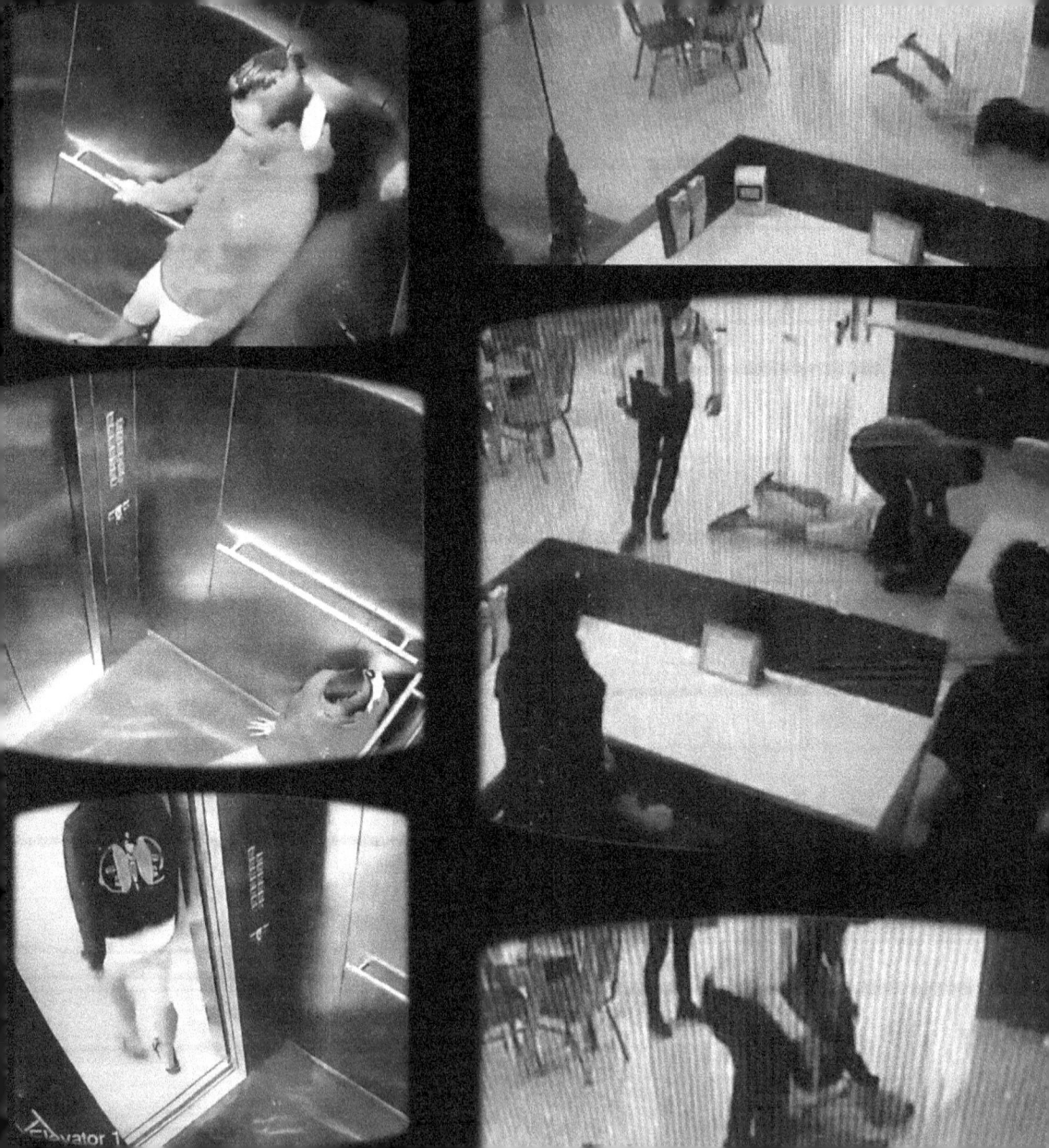

Misaligned

This chapter took me a long time to write, not because it happened long ago, but because it was something I had buried and needed to unearth again. I thought it would be easy since it was in the past, but as they say, the past is never truly forgotten, nor are the pain and struggles that come with it. I'll do my best to keep this straightforward, and I hope it comes across as informative.

I used to thrive in social settings, whether at home or at school. I was genuinely outgoing and had good friends always around me, as far as I can remember. I was there for them when they needed me, and they were there for me too. I put in a lot of effort to keep my relationships strong and steady. I don't recall ever making anyone feel uncomfortable, at least not that I'm aware of, and vice versa. Of course, there were always disagreements and bumps along the way, but things usually worked themselves out over time—especially when a friendship had already been tested.

I belonged to multiple circles: school friends, colleagues, gym buddies, bandmates, and family friends. Gradually, these networks began to overlap. Everyone knew each other; everyone was connected, because I saw no reason to keep them separate.

Then came graduation and the start of facing the real world, where theory and lessons were tested in actual situations, including managing my own finances and being surrounded by people from very different backgrounds. I was assigned to the multimedia department to match my skills, and at first, nothing made me feel out of place. I was learning, interacting smoothly with others, and adapting with confidence and humor. I kept the energy alive in every group, always bringing fun and lightness. Back then, the idea of seeking solitude seemed impossible. I couldn't imagine ever wanting to be alone.

When I transitioned from being a graphic artist to a Pilates instructor, my social landscape naturally changed. The art world connections I once had became less central to my daily life. Although the years we spent together remained valuable memories, my focus gradually shifted to this new path. I met different kinds of people, formed new friendships, and embraced a new environment. I spent more time with instructors, clients, and people who shared similar interests. I loved it, and I told myself that I had finally found the path I was truly meant to follow.

I can't say how my former friends perceive me now. I still communicate with a few of them once in a while. It's just that my comfort zone shifted and eventually became the core of who I am.

As time passed, my friends, coworkers, and family members followed their own paths, many of them moving abroad in search of better opportunities. My sister, brothers, colleagues, and closest friends all set out in new directions. Then, unexpectedly, an opportunity came my way too—a chance to work in a foreign country. Before long, I landed in Singapore.

Even though the excitement grew as the farewell drew near, saying goodbye to everyone wasn't easy, especially to my parents. This new environment promised financial independence and professional growth, but it also meant leaving behind the familiar social ties I had relied on. The first challenge was adjusting to life in my flat, learning to align with housemates whose routines and habits were unfamiliar to me. Outside, I was surrounded by people from different countries who shared ambitions similar to mine, and the differences in appearance, clothing, customs, and beliefs were striking.

Walking through the streets, nothing felt familiar. The language, transportation, buildings, and cuisine felt uncomfortable at first. It was a struggle to learn their cultural norms while holding on to my own. Then, as a normal person would ask:

> *"Is this it? Is it normal to feel this way? Did I make the right decision?"*

At the beginning, it was hard to focus on my goal while being in an unfamiliar environment. The expectations at work felt even more precise than the job itself. During my training and mentorship, I had to adjust my cueing, recognize the subtle gestures of clients, understand tactile guidance, and even refine how I presented myself. It felt like I needed to unlearn everything.

Of course, beyond the intensity of the sixty hours a week I spent working in the studio, there were moments of fun. But sadly, the pressure was constant, and gradually I began to feel something I didn't yet understand. Each day, the internal weight—what I now recognize as anxiety—grew heavier than the lessons I was trying to learn.

The hardest part was that I had no name for it. I didn't know what anxiety was, how it worked, or how to manage it.

> "I didn't know if I needed support, what kind of support that might be, or where to find it, but deep down I knew something wasn't right."

The challenge was compounded by a cultural gap and a language barrier. My boss and coworkers were locals, and they often spoke in their own language. I relied on social cues, but that was never a strength of mine. I was lucky that a close friend lived nearby and worked the same job, so we could spend time together. Even as I grew more familiar with the studio, the city, and my clients, it still wasn't enough to stop the tide of anxiety.

Eventually, the anxiety began to show itself in my body. My social confidence frayed, and my ability to manage work relationships, especially with my boss, declined. We started having disagreements. My performance as an instructor and designer suffered; I could no longer deliver the quality I expected of myself. Every day, my mind kept visualizing negative events, feeding my weaknesses and weighing me down more and more.

"A loop of worst-case scenarios and negative assumptions."

No matter how much my boss tried to support me, I felt beyond repair, or at least that's what I thought. Confusing messages were exchanged. I felt lost and hopeless, yet I kept telling myself to hang on because I was there to learn and become a well-respected Pilates instructor. Entering the studio became harder over time. The moment I closed the door behind me, my voice would disappear:

> "If I tried to speak, the sound that came out was thin and strange, like I had swallowed helium, giving me a Mickey Mouse voice. It was followed by uncontrollable trembling in my hands, with a tingling numbness at the tips of every finger."

I saw clients grow worried and ask if I was ill, and I somehow gave answers to get around their questions. But deep inside, nothing was working, especially as these episodes continued daily. My boss noticed, and it triggered another confrontation. She tried to find common ground and align our expectations, but nothing seemed to work. Perhaps it would have if my mind hadn't already been so unsettled.

Imagine all this happening without me fully understanding why. All I knew then was the discomfort within me: I lost focus, lost sight of my goals, and felt close to losing my mind.

Then things worsened:

> *"I began hearing voices. Laughter echoed from everywhere, a familiar sound that, to my horror, was my own voice."*

It happened when I was in the office one afternoon, working on my designs. It was off-peak; I still remember it was around two o'clock, and the studio was empty. Light and shadow streamed through the windows, the dry, cool air from the air conditioner filled the room, and the only sound was the squeak of my chair. The scene felt eerie, reminding me of when my boss had mentioned that one of the floors was haunted. For a moment, I thought the voices weren't coming from my head at all—that maybe I really was being haunted.

I don't know how I survived those days, but what I do remember is that I went to church every Sunday and prayed every night. I thought it would help with my social and spiritual struggles, but it didn't. The only thought I could hold onto was going back to my motherland, and I did.

The day I was at the airport, waiting for my flight, my mind was in a loop over the thought that I had lost my passport, even though it was right there in my pocket. At the same time, another thought kept repeating: the plane was going to crash. It became four hours of mental torture, created by what I can only describe as my mind's creativity from hell.

> "Imagine how my mind kept backstabbing me, offering no relief and only making the weight heavier as boarding time drew closer."

I somehow observed:

> "Anxiety and excitement feel so similar. Both make you imagine scenarios and quicken your heartbeat, but they translate differently: one brings happiness, the other brings confusion and despair."

But this wasn't my first difficult experience. A few years earlier, I was in a different studio, hoping for more work exposure, training, and mentorship. For the first few months, I felt fine—no stress. But beneath the surface, the same patterns were emerging, mixed with bullying. I didn't expect to work without pay, eat my lunch in the toilet, or watch another trainer break down while speaking to the owner as I taught. The place was full of drama: the receptionist constantly crying, tension in the air, and everyone pushed beyond their limits. I left eventually, but back then, there were no signs of the anxiety that would later follow me. I never thought that pursuing this profession would be dreadful, but despite everything, I never backed down.

Looking back, I realize that social alignment played a huge role in everything, not just in the studio. Every time I stepped into a new environment, I needed to find a balance between myself and the world around me: between my expectations and theirs, between my routines and the culture I was navigating, and between my mind and my body. When that alignment was off, anxiety and struggle followed.

I understand that moving forward isn't about avoiding challenges or never feeling out of place. It's about noticing when I'm out of sync, adjusting, and finding a rhythm that works for me. The challenge is that I'm living it, not observing from the outside. I'm like an actor playing a part with no script.

Alignment became more than a physical practice in Pilates, it became a lens through which I could understand myself, my limits, and the ways I can grow while staying true to who I am. But no matter how I navigate socially or how good the job offer is, I always seem to start from a misaligned point because I struggle to read social cues. And this misalignment doesn't just appear at work, during migration, or under social pressure; it also hits me whenever I'm unprepared, vulnerable, or disoriented.

It first happened back in 2020 when I went home to my country for a three-week holiday.

> "As always, it usually starts with a feeling of confusion and the difficulty of distinguishing between excitement and anxiety, along with visions that mix precaution with tragedy."

But because there were many stopovers, I was lucky to have time to settle my mind—sleeping at the airport and calmly setting aside those mental struggles for the meantime. At the same time, it was continuous mental torture, as anxiety flared every time boarding was announced.

> "A piece of advice: avoid watching airplane accident documentaries before you travel, especially if you have anxiety—something I, unfortunately, always do. I remember one time when I was left alone on the plane during an anxiety attack. The flight attendants helped me regain calmness with their reassuring words and by giving me water, until they allowed me to step off. It was incredibly embarrassing, and they even asked if I wanted an ambulance."

When I arrived home, just after getting off the plane, everything felt overwhelming—the change in temperature, the familiar yet unfamiliar sounds, quietly loud, mixed with the confusing movement all around me: passengers, workers, drivers, and cars coming from different directions. From waiting at the pickup point all the way to the hotel, I was close to having an anxiety attack. But perhaps I was just too tired from traveling, and dozed off as soon as I arrived at the hotel.

That morning, when I woke up,

> "I had no idea my anxiety was still there, hiding in the corner, unnoticed, just waiting for me to awaken."

It even waited while I was enjoying my breakfast. I took a shower, and then, suddenly, everything felt strange. My body started feeling weightless, my hands felt numb and shaky, my vision blurred, and my hearing faded.

The next thing I knew, I was awakened by my sister's voice in the emergency room, looking around while my vision was still struggling to find focus. I was surrounded by a doctor, nurses, and a few others. Confusion set in as I tried to take in the unfamiliar environment and faces, with questions and comforting words coming at me from every direction. It took about an hour, I think, before I regained full control and focus, and only then did I learn that the hotel staff had brought me there after I collapsed in the hotel lobby.

The next day, I went back to the hotel and asked the security staff for the CCTV footage, eager to see what had happened since I couldn't remember anything. I was in shock and completely confused as I watched the footage from behind the counter. On the screen, there I was, leaving my room, moving like a drunk person, dragging myself down the empty hallway. I saw myself press the elevator button and lean beside it, just to stay upright.

The next scene showed me already inside the elevator:

> "I was swaying and fighting to keep my balance, my head repeatedly hitting the corner again and again while I tried to hold myself up."

I couldn't believe that was me—as if someone else was controlling my body. Then the doors slid open. I stumbled out, my right shoulder slamming into the frame. The third footage showed the lobby.

> "My legs were barely moving, as if they refused to bend at the knees—walking in baby steps across the floor, as though they no longer belonged to me."

And then, all at once, I went down in a heavy fall, my head striking the concrete with sickening force. Security rushed toward me, one lifting me up while the other brought a wheelchair. They carried my limp body and rushed me to the ambulance. The impact alone looked painful, even without sound. In a way, the silence made it worse—it left room for my imagination to fill in the pain, adding details that weren't even there.

On the third day, I sat opposite my doctor impatiently while he reviewed my X-ray and a few medical records from the hospital. He calmly explained that, aside from a fractured left orbital wall, which caused nerve damage affecting my taste and smell, I was fortunate to have turned my head and avoided losing any teeth in the fall. Beyond those findings, he couldn't pinpoint exactly why it had happened. The best he could guess was that I might have been dehydrated and experienced a random epileptic episode, since he didn't have my complete medical history. And even if he had, I have no record of anything like that ever happening.

But I wanted to tell the doctor that maybe it was the travel anxiety that caused it. At the time, though, I wasn't sure if it really was part of my anxiety. On top of that, I was also thinking about the excitement and nervousness of meeting someone I'd been talking to online for a month before my holiday. I just wasn't comfortable enough to admit that to my doctor. Still, the same images looped through my head: all the possible scenarios of what might happen, or not. We were supposed to meet on the second day after my arrival.

Even though I don't have a full recollection of that day, it still haunts me because there was no closure and no thorough medical explanation. It still makes me wonder to this day:

> "Who was really 'in charge' during the times I can't remember? Was it my subconscious stepping in while my conscious self went offline? How does that even work?"

> "Is it possible for another part of my mind to take over without me knowing? Or does it only happen when it's needed? Could this 'takeover' happen on normal days without me noticing?"

> "Did I experience something similar to sleepwalking?"

I wished I were one of those lucky individuals who became geniuses after a head trauma. But sadly, my brain gave me nothing more than stubborn anxiety.

After that first episode, the anxiety never struck me as strongly again. Perhaps I had learned enough to handle overwhelming moments. Still, it returned once, in a milder form, during my time in New Zealand. It began the same way as before, with overthinking that escalated into anxiety. The episode caught me by surprise as I was teaching.

> "Again, my hands went numb and shaky, my vision and hearing narrowed, but because I was teaching, my speech was affected. I struggled to find the words. Eventually, I went offline, and something else seemed to take over."

The next thing I remember, I was in another room, lost and shaken. I knew then that I had an attack, especially when one of my clients approached me and asked if I was okay. I had no choice but to be honest and said, "I'm sorry, I had an anxiety attack." After she left, all I could do was burst into silent tears, wishing I hadn't exposed myself so much.

Despite these major setbacks in my Pilates journey and life, most of it has been sweet. I became very attuned to every curve in my Pilates practice, aware of the contrast with anxiety. I was always chasing good results, leveling up my standards, and building a strong foundation to preserve quality.

How my anxiety develops in stages:

These levels are not based on any medical scale, but on my own observations of how anxiety unfolds in my body and mind.

Anxiety Level 1

- Overthinking the "what ifs" during off-work hours
- Lasts about 3–5 days

Anxiety Level 2

- The "what ifs" turn into a series of mental images, mostly negative scenarios
- The intrusive thoughts occur during on- and off-work hours
- Noticeable fidgeting (shaking of legs)
- Increased urination
- Dandruff becomes noticeable

- Lasts around 3 days

Anxiety Level 3

- Mental images loop repeatedly, creating muscle tension (usually around the shoulders and neck)
- Intrusive thoughts occur during on- and off-work hours, also affecting sleep
- Breathing becomes short and shallow
- Feet and hands become numb, the latter sometimes shaking uncontrollably
- Lasts about 30 minutes to an hour, depending on intensity
- Selective memory upon recovery, often followed by crying or emotional confusion

Note: *Anxiety Levels 2 and 3 are interchangeable, depending on the situation or trigger.*

Anxiety Level 4

- Tunnel vision
- Hearing fades
- Breathing becomes short and shallow
- Voice feels shallow (soft, "Mickey Mouse" quality)
- Sensation of lightness in the body
- Sometimes hear voices or laughter; often my own breathing, voice, or my client's voice, depending on where I am
- Lasts around 5–10 minutes
- Patchy memory upon recovery

Anxiety Level 5

- Consciousness switches off
- The body continues the task without awareness
- Duration depends on the task at that moment
- No memory upon recovery

When it comes to relationships, both my anxiety and ASD play an important role. I think it helps me find other ways to connect with people, since my social cue recognition is limited. If you ask me how I identify chemistry or connection, here are the markers I've learned to recognize:

- A back-and-forth exchange of pleasant, meaningful communication over time
- Frequent meet-ups
- Personal topics that come naturally during those meet-ups, and I feel we're aligned

> "Most of the time, I can't really tell if it's friendship or something more, so I just see where it's heading unless they literally tell me so."

Imagine going out with someone and being the only one who thinks it's a date. Of course, it turns awkward the moment I hint at my assumptions, and that's usually where it ends.

> "I can't count how many times I've found myself in this shameful and embarrassing situation."

Here are some examples from my dating experiences:

It was raining when we found ourselves in a café in a small town, just a few minutes' drive from where I live. While she was talking, sitting in front of me, I was observing the movement of her pupils, listening and translating the tone of her voice, while my thoughts were flooded with the pre-scenarios I was trying to align with the real one. I was also trying to carry on a good conversation, all while attempting to calm my anxiety.

I think it went well because, over time, we crossed that unfamiliar stage until she felt comfortable enough to suggest a sleepover at her place. After that conversation, the scenarios kept rolling through my head—thoughts of what might happen and how I'd respond. It went on nonstop throughout the days leading to the sleepover. Of course, by the time that day came, my mind was already so overworked and exhausted that the only thing I wanted was a simple, comfortable sleepover—just to get it over with.

That very night, I lay beside her, trying to avoid any tiring topics that reflected the pre-scenarios I had imagined. She asked if I only wanted to talk. I said yes, and after a few light exchanges, we simply went to sleep until morning.

Another date with a different person started the same way as the first example—my observations, looping thoughts, and so on. I said I wanted to go home since it was past midnight and I needed to get back to my campervan. But she politely asked if I wanted to cuddle. At that moment, I felt surprised; I didn't expect it, and my mind wasn't prepared. So my mouth automatically said yes, while my mind stayed confused. I had no reason to say no, and in my head, I kept thinking it was just a cuddle anyway.

But here's the problem: while driving the 25 minutes to her house, my mind had the opportunity to overthink, again creating pre-scenario sets. By the time we arrived, I was already mentally exhausted. Of course, we just cuddled. I acted as oblivious as always while looking around the unfamiliar room. The decoration, the colors—they just made me more anxious. Then she asked if I knew what cuddling really meant. By then, I learned what it truly involved. And again, as embarrassing as it could get, I talked my way out. I never slept that night, thinking about what I'd done to embarrass myself and embarrass her. Despite all that, I'm glad it turned out to be a lovely evening because she was a genuinely lovely person too.

> "Why isn't my mind flexible enough to adapt to changes? Why is it so stubborn about going along with the situation—as if I can only act according to what I'm pre-programmed to do?"

> "I think this might be one of those reasons health professionals say that being literal is a trait of ASD. To me, however, being literal feels more like the result of mental exhaustion—especially in situations like the one above."

I still can't wrap my head around the fact that I might have literally been told what to do beforehand in all my past relationships. It makes me feel broken in ways I can't explain, because these people were amazing. I can hardly stand to think about what I've done, especially now that I need to remember every detail so I can write it down.

That is why, after so many years, I've chosen this single path: because it saves me from hating myself.

Why I prefer physical interaction in relationships:

1. Clarity over ambiguity
   Physical connection is immediate and predictable, unlike social cues or emotional subtleties, which often require guessing and can be exhausting for me.

2. Confidence in interaction
   Touch, presence, and movement provide a clear way to engage, allowing me to feel naturally connected without overthinking every response.

3. Non-verbal understanding
   I can sense affection, care, or curiosity through observation—the tilt of one's head, their tone of voice, or eye contact—even though interpreting social cues doesn't come automatically to me.

4. Energy conservation
   Focusing on physical aspects reduces mental overload, letting me enjoy closeness without the fatigue that constant social interpretation often brings.

5. Emotional resonance

    Even without words or conventional social cues, I can experience love, connection, and empathy through physical presence alone.

That is why my first marriage began with misalignment and eventually fell into chaos, and why the second one gradually shifted into friendship. Relying primarily on the physical aspect to connect seems simple at first, but I've realized it's not enough to sustain a relationship—it can only take you so far.

"Does the absence of social cues put you in danger?"

I think it can, specifically with this story I'm about to share. A terrifying experience from my younger years unfolded on what seemed like a typical Friday night. I was hanging out with a friend at his resto-bar when I met someone who seemed sweet and looked the part. We seemed to have good chemistry and connection, so I ended up driving her home.

When I woke up, my phone contacts had vanished, my cash had disappeared, and I found myself locked inside the house with her. Panic gripped me, and I begged her to let me go, but she just laughed. I feared it was the end of me. Luckily, someone—maybe her flatmate—arrived, and I seized the chance to escape.

I consider myself lucky too, because my anxiety didn't intrude at that moment. Perhaps, like me, my anxiety was still too young to take over the situation.

Looking back now, I realize that some of these experiences may have been amplified by my difficulty reading social cues—and, of course, my persistent anxiety. I also think my mind will never fully learn lessons from them, because it's not wired that way. I hope the only way to navigate my life is to gain a deeper understanding of my literal thinking, study the patterns of my past, and be cautious of my own boundaries to avoid creating shameful and embarrassing moments.

Lines guide, connect, and shape everything, visible or invisible, natural or man-made.

Reading the World

My world, as I've described, isn't very wide. It mostly revolves around van life, work, and business. I also have a habit of pursuing particular interests during my off-peak hours. The one that dominated my attention for about three years was religion. I took courses on Christianity, scriptures, and comparative religion, eventually diving into theology. More recently, I shifted my focus to painting, spending most of my time on commissions. After that, I started working on this book.

During breaks from whatever interest occupied me at the time, I swam regularly. Now, I'm drawn to short hikes, spending roughly 45 minutes to an hour hiking the same mountain path three days a week. Since I walk this route regularly, I sometimes notice how my brain perceives vision. For example, when I'm ascending a section of the trail where I can't see the horizon or sky, it often feels like I'm going downhill instead of uphill.

The only indicator that I'm actually climbing is my labored breathing. And when I'm descending with the sea and horizon in the background,

> "It feels as if I'm standing at the edge of a waterfall, about to fall straight through."

As I've previously mentioned, I wonder if our minds ever really know whether we're dreaming or in a simulation, because the mind can simply create its own version of reality.

As I walk, I keep noticing how everything around me appears both random and yet defined by lines—the footpath, the gravel and rocks, the stairs and the drainage system, the bushes and trees, the fences and signage, as well as the shadows they cast. Even the sheep, especially their wool, seem to hold lines that mark every detail. When I look up, the pattern continues. Whether it's clouds, rain, paragliders, or airplanes, everything seems to carry or be shaped by lines. This observation follows me everywhere I go.

When I'm on the highest peak and take in the beautiful view—the waves, the surfers, the cargo ships, yachts, fishing boats—I start to wonder:

> "If the waves created by these vessels didn't form a lined pattern, could we still see them?"
>
> "If the clouds didn't cast shadows over the sea, could we still notice the contrast of colors?"
>
> "If lines didn't matter in designing these vessels, would they even float?"
>
> "And if architecture didn't consider lines as part of a house's beauty and function, what would our cities look like?"
>
> "If bridges didn't have lines in their structural design, would they even be safe to cross?"

Even if we break down architecture, slabs, frame supports, beams, nails, and screws are all arranged along lines. The same goes for tension cables, bolts, and beams in bridges. Taking all of this together, you have to wonder:

"How is it that everything seems shaped and arranged along lines?"

"Why are lines the foundation of creation, whether in nature or in human design?"

Even the invisible lines we can't see in the physical world follow patterns. Technology is full of them. Every house, every commercial building, every mode of transportation and nearly every person interacting with them is connected through lines—networks, signals, systems. Even the Wi-Fi icon is illustrated as a series of radiating lines.

Lines guide, connect, and shape everything, whether visible or invisible, natural or human-made. If we look to nature, many species rely on invisible lines too: sound waves, sonar, and other signals to communicate and navigate their world. From the precise alignment of ants to the geometric structure of a beehive to geese flying in V-formation, lines and patterns are everywhere. I assume these are governed by instinctive rules; ours are simply more complex due to scale and proportion.

This principle extends to written contracts and social rules. Laws are numbered in sequence, lawmakers are arranged by position, and law enforcement officers are organized in ranks. For everything to work, it all operates through patterned systems.

> "Sometimes I wonder if this is even worth asking: why do we need a brain to create lines with purpose when nature, without any brain at all, already does it better?"

And because I was raised and lived as a Christian man, I can't help but ask if there really is a creator responsible for these deliberate lines in nature. There's been an endless debate about this, one that's never been resolved, whether between religion and science, between denominations, or across parallel belief systems. When I look around, I see how each person's religion aligns with their geography and is molded by their culture, much like the social rules we construct. If civil laws exist, so do divine laws, numbered in sequence and governed by religious leaders organized in hierarchies.

The similarities don't end there. When I bring my curiosity to the divine world as described in the holy book, I find the same foundation of lines. It's as if there's no difference from the natural world. From the stairway to heaven to the pearly gates, the streets of gold, kingdoms, thrones, clothes, and the divine beings occupying them, everything is formed and shaped by lines.

And since we're already discussing things in our skies, that raises another set of questions. Why not consider UAPs (unidentified aerial phenomena)? There are countless sources about them online: written documents, photos, videos, and illustrations. Whether they're true or not, I can't help wondering why these things seem to adhere to geometric forms. Whether it's a craft or an alien spy drone, occupied or autonomous, how come they also seem to be built on lines as a foundation? Again, it's as if our so-called primitive planet is no different from an alien one.

If I use my imagination about life from other galaxies, I wouldn't assume their definition of life is similar to ours, or that they're shaped and formed by lines at all. Because most of these beings, as drawn by witnesses, are shown standing upright with similar anatomical arrangements—familiar facial features and hands that appear to function just like ours—they feel more like distant cousins than beings from an alien planet. I can't help but laugh a little while wondering, even just in my imagination, whether these aliens also evolved from crawling creatures to upright ones, just as we did.

I hope that one day I'm still here when we finally begin to solve these unsettling mysteries in our skies, since they live out there among the stars glowing above us.

Those same stars have captured our imagination in different ways. In my case, when I was a kid, I thought the stars were comets. They all looked the same to me, just tiny glowing dots in the sky. I even imagined their purpose was to light up the night. In a way, they do. But the value we place on stars varies: some people don't care about them at all, while others spend their lives studying them. I think about how stars order themselves, and how we name their patterns according to shapes and alignments we see—the zodiac constellations like Aries and Cancer, or mythical figures like Orion and Crux. Most ancient civilizations used these alignments for navigation or mapping their gods onto the heavens. The stars above might be scattered randomly, but I like to think our minds saw that randomness as an invitation to find meaning.

Sometimes I find myself wondering about the ancient Greek philosophers and observers, the ones who first noticed these alignments in the skies.

> *"Were they also neurodivergent, like me?"*

> *"Did they see patterns in ways others didn't?"*

And because autism hadn't been identified back then,

> *"Could it be that people simply called them the sky-watchers of their time?"*

It's obvious to me that we can only shape what's above according to what we observe from below.

> "Sometimes I think the stars don't really teach us anything new, maybe it's us who teach ourselves, framing everything beyond us within the limits of our own minds."

If beings from other worlds exist, I imagine they'd have their own interpretations of the skies above them too. If I were sent back in time and the Babylonians or Greeks put me in their sky-watchers department, I'm sure the zodiac would include a mobile phone, hiking boots, a campervan, a dog, a fruit ice-cream, and Jesus Christ—things that I can actually relate to. And since there are countless stars available to form patterns, I wonder:

> "Does the same pattern-seeking apply when walking along a sandy, gravelly hiking path?"

Yes, because the countless tiny stones and pebbles on the ground can also be arranged into whatever patterns we want.

You might also wonder if I have an obsession with lines.

I don't think so. I have neither the urge nor any sense of compulsion. In fact, I never believed it affected my life—I used to think everything that happened was simply part of my path. But after my diagnosis, my perspective shifted.

Perhaps the best example of true obsession can be seen in the Nazca Lines in Peru. I've never been there, but it's where ancient people carved gigantic images of animals, geometric figures, and lines across mountains—so large they can only be seen from the air. Compared to that scale, my preoccupations seem like nothing. It's fascinating that the ancient world left us with geometric structures and line drawings everywhere—cave paintings, pyramids, ground markings, star alignments—as their ways of reading their world. And now we have filled our entire world with lines.

It's not just that I notice lines everywhere I look. Imagine going to a Pilates studio where no lines mark the mat or define the reformer's frame. How could anyone have a proper workout if the equipment itself wasn't clearly delineated? Imagine a dance studio with no corners or boundaries defining the floor, or an indoor climbing wall with no lines shaping the holds. Even the movements we use to stay fit seem to follow lines in one way or another.

Lines also seem to appear in the forces of nature. I've never been close to a tsunami, but it seems as if those rushing waters are made of lines, moving with an invisible order as they reshape everything in their path. Earthquakes leave cracks, sinkholes, and patterns in the earth's surface, all traced by lines formed from shifting tectonic plates. Even a simple scratch on a wall creates lines. Hurricanes, tornadoes, typhoons, and sandstorms all carry lines in the way they move and take shape.

> "How would we separate ourselves from each other if there were no borders, houses, roads, towns, cities, islands, or continents?"

> "How could we even navigate without paths, connecting flights, roads, or maps?"

> "In a world without lines, not only would existence itself fade, but even the spirit world—the realm of every god ever worshipped, seated upon thrones shaped by lines—might not survive without them."

How my hyper-observation functions in everyday situations:

1. Patterns in behavior
   I notice sequences in everyday tasks, like the way I eat or arrange objects, and it feels more satisfying when things follow an order.

2. Attention to detail
   Subtle sensory cues—textures, flavors, or visual arrangements—stand out in ways that might not register to most people.

3. Cause-and-effect awareness
   I can sense how certain foods, routines, or environments affect my body and mind.

4. Observation of the world
   I notice patterns and order in my surroundings—from chefs plating dishes to how animals move—and often reflect on why things are done that way.

5. Integration with decision-making
   These observations guide my understanding, decisions, and creativity, helping me navigate the world more intentionally.

Arnel_Gaviola

Reflection and Insight

When I was driving back to town after my diagnosis, so many things were running through my head. It was confusing, surprising, even a bit shocking, because I had no idea something like that existed beyond what I already knew about myself. I thought I was simply dealing with anxiety and depression caused by migration. I kept digging through all the memories I could recall, trying to identify which parts were truly me and which might be shaped by ASD.

It was a lot to take in. Even after I got home from work, it stayed on my mind—I just couldn't fully process it. I shared it with my siblings and close friends, hoping for some clarity, but everyone had a different opinion. What I really needed then was a sense of certainty, something that could convince me that I had autism, or at least help me come to terms with it. ASD felt like a silent, subtle condition. I kept wondering how it could be a disorder if I could function well, stay organised, and keep working toward my goals. I had always thought a disorder meant something obvious, something that looked completely different from what I considered normal behavior.

So I thought it might be better to research more about ASD, since at that point I couldn't step back from my thoughts to observe myself clearly. I Googled it, watched videos on YouTube, but the more time I spent researching, the more confused I became. What I realized, though, was that this journey is deeply personal and every person's experience on the spectrum is different. I felt like I was back to square one, unable to move forward, unsure of what I was really looking for, and not even knowing where to begin.

On Campervan

Ever since I started living in my van, my creativity has sparked brighter than ever. Ideas come more easily, and new creative projects seem to find their way to me. Everything in my mind feels smoother, as if planning and imagining have become effortless.

The van isn't just a home—it's a space that supports my focus, calm, and imagination.

Off Medication

My focus with ASD has never been on finding a cure, because there isn't one. Instead, it's about managing my anxiety, which I'm gradually getting better at.

> "The tricky thing about anxiety is that even when you find a method to contain it, it often finds another way to sneak in."

It's like a living organism: you think you've killed it, but it just evolves. I can only outsmart it once before it shifts its strategy. I guess it's a lifetime game of cat and mouse.

I've been taking medication for years, and every year I test myself to see if I'm truly stable by stopping my meds for a month. Sometimes I feel hopeful, thinking maybe it has already left me.

But do you know what I experience during those months without medication? Fatigue. An uneasy feeling. Crying every night for no reason. And illusions when I close my eyes before sleep.

If you're wondering about the illusions, they're vivid and strange. They are:

- Sometimes in white italic font—similar to the kind you'd find on birthday cakes set against a black fabric backdrop
- Other times, a light gray, unfinished concrete wall
- Sometimes random words in gold, brushstroke lettering on a textured stone wall

Even now, I'm not entirely sure if, during those moments, I'm already asleep or still fully awake—because in my mind, I feel completely conscious.

> "I think that no matter what medication I take to balance my hormones or suppress anxiety, if that's even how it works, no complex compound made from material in the outside world can truly reach the conscious mind to untie the knots that cause it. For me, medication

is not about unraveling those knots, because it never will. It's about somehow convincing my conscious brain that it helps."

On Painting

Then one day—I forget the reason, maybe out of boredom—I went to an art shop to buy painting materials: paintbrushes, acrylic paints, and a canvas. I watched some YouTube videos to relearn the basics, since it had been about twenty years since I last painted. When I began, I noticed that my mind stopped wandering. Painting also quieted the endless questions and visions swirling within me.

Back in my university days, my focus was only on the result, it had nothing to do with what was going on in my mind. But this time, it felt different. After a few weeks, every time I finished a commission and delivered it to the owner, I felt a deep sense of relief. Every painting I've done brought me a sense of peace.

Then I realized it wasn't the painting itself that calmed my mind, but the focus I put into it. And it worked well, especially since one of the traits of ASD is difficulty with multitasking—in this case, that limitation became an advantage. Sometimes I wonder why creativity slows down my mind in a good way. Maybe it's because creativity and ASD have something in common: both were part of me long before I even knew it.

I think that no matter how hard a painter tries to capture sadness or depression, it never appears raw or unformed. Instead, it always emerges as something shaped, something framed, something alive. I've realized that the raw, unfiltered weight of sorrow or fear in our minds can never truly be reproduced on canvas. Even when I mix colors to express it, the pigments themselves bring life and movement to the piece.

> "So when my mind starts to wander, it sets the stage for anxiety later. Doing something I've loved for as long as I can remember seems to help prevent it, or at least slows it down before it takes over."

On Music

As I mentioned earlier, I'm musically inclined, and music has a calming effect on me, as it does for many others. People are drawn to musical instruments for various reasons. I'm particularly interested in the violin, cello, and saxophone.

Listening to music gives me a feeling similar to being with pets—the music tells a solemn story in my head. It's actually a big turnaround for me, as I've never really listened to instrumental music before. I'm not into loud, heavy metal either; I lean more toward alternative music, like Morrissey or The Cure, and, more recently, Sam Smith.

I also listen to foreign-language ballads where I don't understand a single word. Sometimes I prefer this because the melody alone carries its own story inside my head, and I find myself completely captivated by it. I don't mind songs I can understand either, it's just that my mind gets distracted by the lyrics, and it starts to feel more like watching a movie, where the focus shifts from the melody to the songwriter's story.

And if you want to know about the visions in my mind whenever I listen to those genres, they come from movies, especially Korean dramas I've watched. Those beautiful, dramatic scenes replay in my mind as if they belong to the real world, as if they were moments I could step into. I think we all go through this phase at some point in life; maybe I'm just still stuck in mine.

On Sounds

Background noise plays an important role when you're autistic. We tend to pick up sounds randomly in nature and also in crowded places, like restaurants, especially in moments when anxiety starts to build. It's not always like that, though. If I've been to the same place a few times, it usually gets easier. It's as if my brain learns to process things ahead of time.

Early signs that my brain is starting to overload from background noise include jaw clenching, shoulder tension, and a headache.

That's why, as I mentioned earlier, melodic and ballad songs help calm my mind. They create a rhythm and softness that restores balance when everything else feels too loud.

I believe the combination of unwelcome sounds and unfamiliar crowd movement was the main cause of my collapse when I went home in 2020. My mind became so overloaded that it could no longer process everything—it simply shut down.

When it comes to interactions, the tone of voice matters deeply to me. A voice that sounds like a ballad or carries a melodic softness helps calm my mind in the same way music does. When people speak at a slower pace, with a gentle tone, it makes a big difference—I can process their words more clearly, and it brings a sense of calm.

There's something about that kind of voice—fragile, peaceful, harmless, and caring—that feels safe. And when it's matched with a gentle smile or a light laugh, everything feels secure.

On Technology

I suppose having ASD often comes with its close companions: anxiety and sometimes depression. I'm not entirely sure if I've ever truly experienced depression. I mean, we all go through moments of feeling low at some point, but that's different from the kind of darkness that makes someone want to give up. There was a time when I pictured myself standing near a train—not because I wanted to end my life, but more as a passing image, a thought without intent or emotion behind it. I suppose that distinction is important. These days, only two things make me feel truly depressed:

> *"Animal cruelty and seeing an electric scooter lying on the pavement."*

Of course, no one with a heart can stand to see animals being treated badly, that's why I usually block or skip those videos when they appear on my feed. But what I can't block or skip is the sight of a fallen scooter. Some might find this observation strange or even funny, but for me, it feels deeply emotional. In my mind,

> "It's as if the scooter has been left alone to die on the pavement while people just walk past as if its 'death' doesn't matter at all."

I even get the urge to pick it up, though most of the time I see them while I'm driving. I don't fully understand why I feel this way.

> "It's similar to how I feel when I see robotic vacuum cleaners or lawn cutters—these machines are given tasks to perform, yet no consciousness to complain."

There's something about that that feels unbearably sad to me.

> "Maybe what I feel isn't really about the scooter or the machines themselves—it's probably a reflection of something in me. Or maybe I'm just overly empathetic in a very particular way."

I've seen many tragic events in my life: accidents, sickness, conflicts, even natural deaths, but somehow, I think we humans are smart enough to handle them. We know how to take care of ourselves and express our feelings in so many ways. That's why the sadness I feel toward humans, animals, and these technologies are three completely different things.

On Animals

The other thing that prevents my mind from wandering is, strangely, looking into the eyes of certain animals, such as guinea pigs, rabbits, sheep, cows, horses, cats, and especially dogs.

Why?

> "I don't feel uncomfortable looking them in the eye—in fact, the eyes are the first thing I seek every time I meet one of these lovely creatures."

It's as if I have the confidence to break the invisible barrier between us, and somehow, it just dissolves. I feel that these gentle beings allow me to see them as they truly are, without any explanation or exchange whatsoever. The longer I stare into their eyes, the more I feel drawn in, as if my social senses can understand what they feel inside. It's like a silent message telling me how fragile they are, how much they need to be cared for.

> "Perhaps I find animals less draining because their behavior is straightforward—their social cues are simple, nonverbal, and honest. There's no guessing or decoding involved, no hidden tone or expression to interpret."

I often feel emotional, especially when I see geese and ducks at the pond. In my mind, I can't help but think how sad it must be to live in this world without hands, to rely entirely on a beak for everything: eating, grooming, protecting, and raising their young. That same beak has to do it all. Meanwhile, some creatures are given sharp teeth, claws, strength, and power to dominate and hunt others that were simply created as their prey. And not one of them ever had a choice in how they were created.

> "All men are created equal, but not all animals are."

On Mountains

All my hiking experiences are fun, especially when I'm with a group. It's just that the process isn't always easy—and I'm not talking about the physical preparation or training, because that part is manageable. It's the one thing I can't train: my mind. Certain heights trigger my anxiety, and I don't always know why. It usually starts with a familiar progression: cold hands, then numb feet that feel as if they're floating above the ground, followed by narrowing vision and tight breathing. In those moments, my mind floods with the same specific questions every time.

> "What if I die here? Who's going to rescue me?"

And, as crazy as it sounds, I counter my anxious brain with this specific thought as well.

> "It's just in my head."

But of course, my anxious brain always wins. It's simply stronger than my reasoning. So I usually take a short break, focus on my breathing, and once it settles a bit, I move on. How I wish there were a "mind gym" where people struggling mentally could just sit on a chair, wear a complex helmet connected to a machine, and train their minds to withstand the unpredictable challenges waiting along the path.

In contrast to those mental struggles, there's something else that makes me smile when I hike. Because the trail is usually quiet, every sound becomes easier to notice—the rustle of leaves, birds chirping above the branches, even the soft crunch of sand and gravel underfoot. I find myself paying attention to the little conversations around me too: a mother telling her child they're almost there, preteens talking about Ariana Grande, teenagers laughing about someone they dated, women sharing stories about stressful relationships, and older hikers who don't say much, just smile and greet as they pass. Listening to all of this keeps my mind busy and makes me aware of how different everyone's journey is. In those moments, I realise that every walk of life really is different.

On Beaches

I usually hang out at the beach about three times a week, not so much by choice, but because that's where most of the camper van parking spots are. And honestly, even though I was born in a tropical country, there are a few things I don't always find relaxing about the beach. I can't even take a nap or close my eyes like other people I see there, especially when:

- It's so sunny, almost like summer, that the brightness becomes distracting. I'm not talking about the heat, because that part is manageable. It's the light itself that overwhelms me, almost like a car's headlight flashing in front of me but magnified a billion times.
- The waves get so strong that the white ridges that form and overlap become uncomfortable to look at. It reaches a point where I don't know where to rest my eyes, and it just feels distracting.
- The sound becomes layered and can be just as intense. Overlapping waves mean overlapping noises, each with a different pitch and volume, creating a jumble that can be hard to filter out.

But that doesn't mean I hate going to the beach. I still enjoy and love it, just for a different purpose. I often compare the feeling to that of a dog: the excitement they show when they're there, chasing birds, running in the shallow water, or playing ball with their owner. I've never seen a dog just chilling on the beach, taking a nap. Perhaps, like me, they see it as more of a playground than a place to relax.

> "Sunrise and sunset at low tide, as well as time spent by lakes and rivers, are a different story. Those are more my preference, offering a true sense of mental rejuvenation."

On Questions

This constant need for details and clarity asking questions, struggling to connect when information is missing—is rooted in my ASD.

- My brain naturally seeks completeness and coherence, so missing information feels uncomfortable.

- I process stories, social interactions, and real-life events by breaking them into pieces and making sure every thread fits.
- It's not about impatience or annoyance—it's how I understand the world and the people in it.

Recognizing this pattern in myself helps me see why I've always asked so many questions and why incomplete or ambiguous narratives, whether in movies or documentaries, can feel stressful.

These days, I no longer ask as many questions aloud while watching movies or in everyday situations. Instead, I keep most of my curiosity to myself, especially when it comes to topics that truly capture my interest, like evolution or history. Yet I've written many questions throughout these narratives to show exactly how my mind works, without filtering or holding back, so the account is as authentic and true to my personality and experience with ASD as possible.

On Hyper-Focus

I also have this trait where I can focus on something for hours. As you might have noticed, many of the things I get drawn to share that same pull—even to the point that I want to understand, in my own way, why a black hole is created.

I imagine the universe as a giant foam. Every second, it expands, and to make room for that expansion, it creates holes—and that's where black holes form. The foam, like Einstein's fabric analogy, can bend smoothly, but I feel foam is better because it curves more naturally, allowing planets and stars to follow its shape.

When I think about how stars and planets are born, I picture that same foam stretching and bubbling. The stretched parts become thin and filled with light—the energy that gathers and forms stars. The denser areas compress into the beginnings of planets, shaped by the same outward push that drives the universe to grow. In this way, creation and collapse happen together, like the foam breathing—one side forming light, the other deepening into darkness.

To explore this idea further, I even asked ChatGPT to turn it into a mathematical equation—even though I don't understand every number in it. For me, it's not about being "correct" but about giving shape to imagination.

The Foam Universe Equation

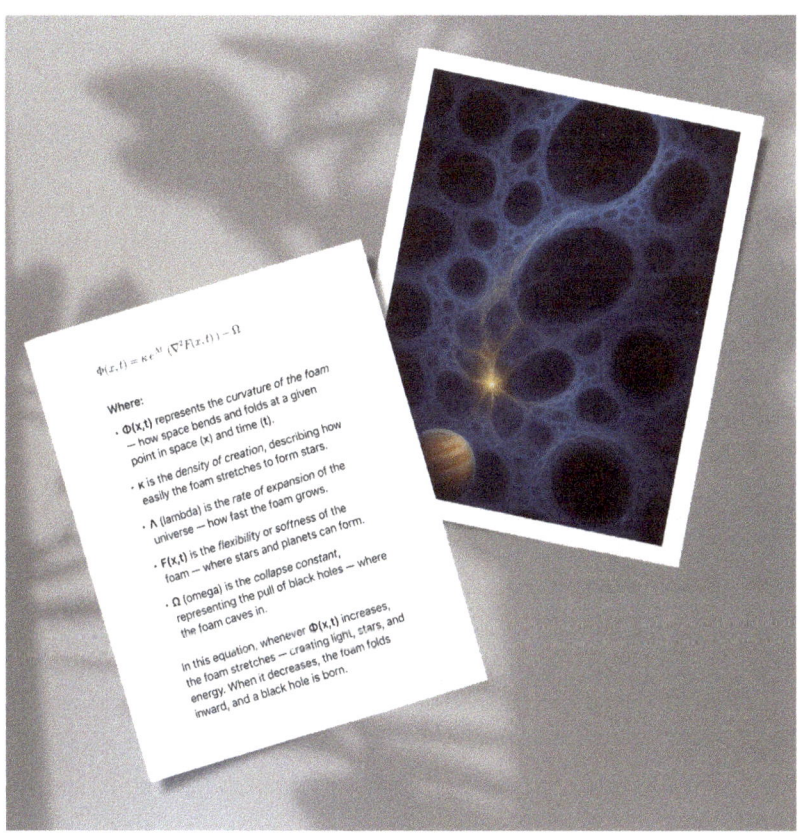

$$\Phi(x,t) = \kappa e^{\Lambda t} (\nabla^2 F(x,t)) - \Omega$$

Where:

- $\Phi(x,t)$ represents the curvature of the foam — how space bends and folds at a given point in space (x) and time (t).
- κ is the density of creation, describing how easily the foam stretches to form stars.
- Λ (lambda) is the rate of expansion of the universe — how fast the foam grows.
- $F(x,t)$ is the flexibility or softness of the foam — where stars and planets can form.
- Ω (omega) is the collapse constant, representing the pull of black holes — where the foam caves in.

In this equation, whenever $\Phi(x,t)$ increases, the foam stretches — creating light, stars, and energy. When it decreases, the foam folds inward, and a black hole is born.

In my "foam universe," black holes form wherever expansion is strongest and the foam bends most easily. Where it stretches softly, stars and planets emerge—the universe's own way of growing. I like this idea because it turns my mental image—a soft, bendable foam—into something that can be written and shared, even if it's just my own playful theory.

This equation isn't meant to describe real physics—it's part of my own "foam universe" idea. Think of it as a way to translate my imagination into mathematics: a way to give shape to how I visualize the universe stretching, bubbling, and forming stars and black holes. It's playful and symbolic, not a formula for modeling actual black holes.

Another example of my hyper-focus: I don't just think about the foam theory—I even think about gravity. But since I don't fully understand the science, I understand it differently. Using complicated scientific terms to explain an already complex universe doesn't help me grasp it. I never disliked science; I just find the method of understanding it a bit off-putting. I'm curious, but reading about it often leaves me more confused.

Listening to scientists sometimes helps, but sometimes it only adds more layers I can't connect with.

If you ask me how gravity behaves, I'd say there is no gravity—at least not in the way we're typically told. It's not a force or a curve in space-time—it's something deeper, something tied to awareness. The more aware or intelligent a being is, the "heavier" it becomes. The more ignorant it is, the freer it moves—like ants that crawl along walls, unaware of what "falling" even means. Maybe the universe itself—stars, planets, galaxies—behaves the way it does because it has no awareness of weight, danger, or consequence.

When we were young, we did physically impossible things without hesitation. But as we age and become more aware, we become more careful, weaker, less mobile, less agile. The daring is gone, and we become like rocks—or, as some say, we return to soil. We grow so afraid that we prefer not to move anymore.

This is why I think some scientists or archaeologists don't fully understand how ancient civilizations created those megastructures—using tons of stone blocks made of volcanic rock or granite that even modern machinery struggles to handle. Maybe their understanding of gravity, or awareness itself, was entirely different from ours. That's why they call it "lost technology." Maybe it's not about losing technology at all, but about the birth of awareness.

The more we understand the world, the heavier we feel. Awareness gives us meaning, but also burden. Nature doesn't care who we are; it just is. It doesn't follow our laws of physics because it doesn't know them. The more we define and measure nature, the more we separate ourselves from its flow.

Awareness Gravity Theory:
How Consciousness Shapes the Pull of Reality

I sometimes think of it as a kind of "awareness gravity"—a gravity that doesn't pull masses, but minds. The equation could look something like this:

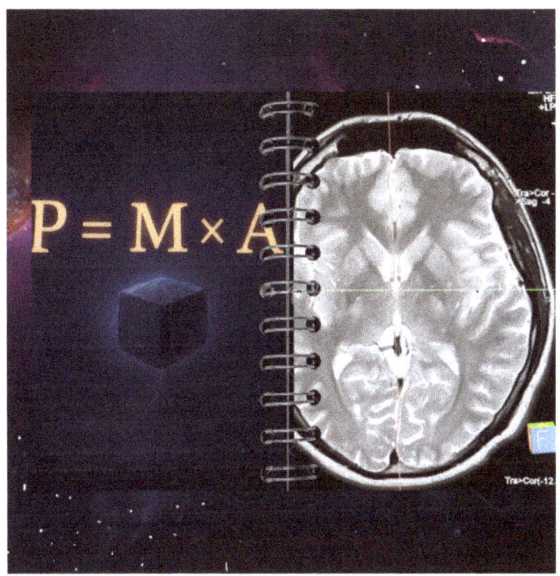

Where P is perceived weight, M is mass, and A is awareness.

As awareness increases, so does the feeling of being "pulled down" by reality.

When awareness is low—like in dust, ants, or stars—there's almost no perceived pull, so they move freely, naturally, without concern.

Hyper-focus feels like escaping that pull. When I'm deeply focused, I lose the weight of awareness—I stop thinking about consequences, time, or even myself. It's like floating in space: no pressure, no resistance, just movement and creation. That's why I think hyper-focus isn't only attention—it's gravity-free awareness.

To be honest, I'm no longer sure if I'm truly artistic—or if I'm just autistic, and creativity is simply part of that. Maybe it's all just how hyper-focus manifests in me. Because not all artists are autistic, but almost every autistic person I've met has some kind of creative pull.

Sometimes I even wonder if creativity is the default mode of autism—a way of communicating when words or logic don't quite fit. I can't tell the difference between simply creating and being hyper-focused anymore, because they overlap so much that I don't think I can separate them.

When I paint, I'm not just making something beautiful; I'm trying to figure something out—like how a black hole forms, or why the universe moves the way it does. Hyper-focus turns into art, and art turns into exploration. It's all part of the same process.

I think being hyper-focused means immersing myself in creating or figuring out something completely outside my knowledge. A good example is the foam theory I mentioned earlier—I spent so much time on it despite having no formal scientific background. Another example is designing and rendering things like a motorcycle, an e-bike, a ground projector GPS, and even a dog collar speaker—projects far removed from my actual knowledge base. I don't know much about engineering or automotive design, yet I spent hours bringing these ideas to life, driven by the need to see how they might look in reality.

On Stimming

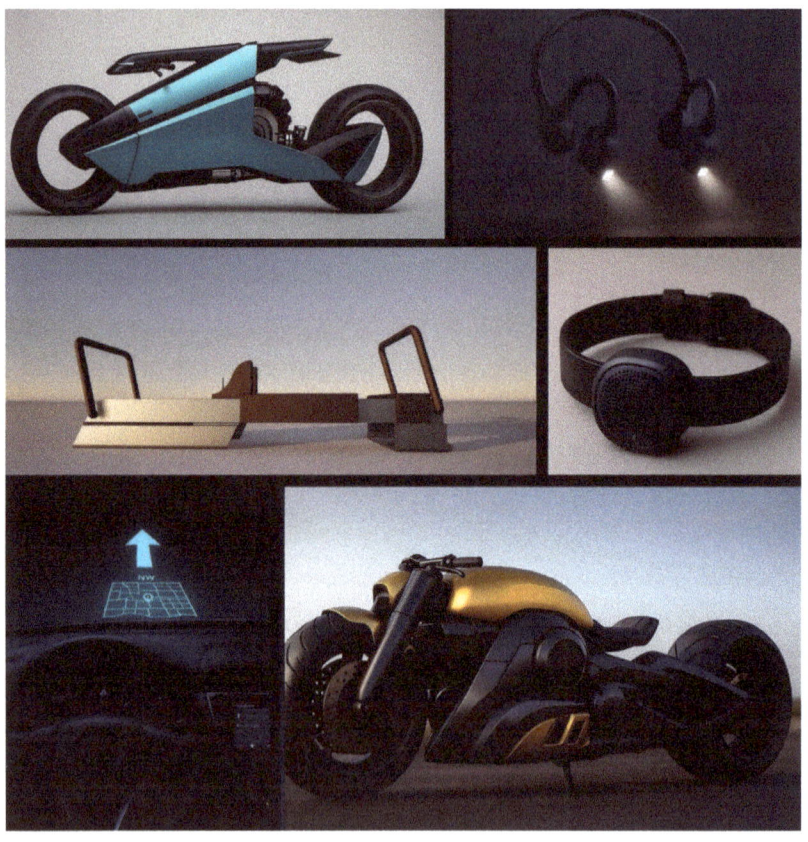

Just as I've always asked questions to make sense of the world, there also are other ways my mind works quietly behind the scenes. Sometimes I trace objects with my fingers or follow their contours with my eyes. Other times, I write words in the air to remember their spelling. I know this might sound unusual, but everyone has their own version of these—tapping a pen, doodling, or moving while thinking.

For me, though, these aren't just habits. They help me process information and focus. My hands and eyes become extensions of my mind, tracing patterns and connecting ideas that I might otherwise miss. They are part of how my mind organizes, understands, and interacts with the world. These small, quiet actions are some of the ways I navigate life and make sense of my thoughts.

I also experience verbal stimming, where I repeat a word over and over in my mind first, and then say it aloud if I'm by myself. Sometimes I even set it to a tune. I know it doesn't serve any practical purpose, and I can't find a logical reason for it, but there's something soothing about hearing the word repeated. I often wonder if there's any meaning behind it—whether my mind is trying to tell me something through the rhythm. There's an inexplicable feeling that comes with it, a kind of quiet satisfaction, as if the sound becomes a pattern that my brain can follow.

The words change all the time, almost like passing thoughts that briefly settle before moving on. Right now, the ones that seem to float around me are Lucy and Göbekli Tepe.

I don't know why these particular words feel right at the moment, but they do. Saying them feels like tracing a melody—familiar, grounding, and oddly peaceful.

On Community

I was invited to a day-and-a-half event hosted by an autism and ADHD community in my city. At first, I was hesitant because I didn't know anyone there, and the biggest group I'd ever been a part of was a religious one, which came with its own struggles and expectations.

I asked a lot of questions beforehand, even inquiring about the age range of attendees, because I didn't want anyone to feel awkward, including myself. I even checked their Facebook page just to get a sense of what to expect.

When the day arrived, I went to the hall and was greeted by a few friendly faces who showed me where to sit. As I walked over, I wasn't listening to anything. I was scanning the whole room, noticing every detail and every unfamiliar face.

Once seated, the first thing that caught my eye was a box of toys they called fidgets. I didn't understand their purpose at first. They looked like little, non-functional toys, things to keep your hands busy. Then I noticed many people around me using them, some examining them, others just turning them over in their hands.

Curious, I tried a few. At first, nothing clicked until I picked up one particular fidget. My hands moved without thinking. My mind felt simultaneously light, focused and calm, as if that small toy was exactly what I needed at that moment. Without realizing it, I had been playing with it for nearly two hours. It was strange—I couldn't explain why it worked, but it did. Later, I found out this experience is called tactile stimming.

What made the experience even more special was that it was the first group I've joined where I felt no pressure—no need to force conversation or make an effort to connect. It was simply easy. There was a program, but it didn't create any stress. Everyone was listening, but it never felt intense. Even when we were divided into smaller groups, the atmosphere stayed calm and open. We were given a few questions to reflect on, but it was completely fine if you didn't want to answer. I found myself more interested in listening, noticing every word people shared. I didn't have to worry about asking the right questions because somehow the answers came naturally through others' contributions.

You could stand, sit, or walk around, and no one minded. It felt like gentle chaos held within an invisible structure—everyone was talking, yet it felt like we were all part of one connected group. I had never experienced anything like it.

You could approach anyone and start a conversation about anything, and it was always okay. It was such an easy, convenient, stress-free environment. Time flew by so fast.

For me, being part of a group like this is so important because I could truly be myself, and so could everyone else. I learned so much: about sensory rooms and what they're for, about why noise cancelling headphones matter, and about the ways each person navigates their life. But I wasn't just learning from others, I was discovering things about myself too.

I never regretted going. And I can't wait to join the next one.

On Masking

Looking back, I realize that many of my traits—asking too many questions, being overly cautious, suppressing my natural reactions—were all part of what's called masking. For most of my life, I tried to appear more "normal," mimicking social behaviors and hiding the parts of me that felt different or misunderstood. I learned to smile when I felt anxious, to stay quiet when something confused me, and to pretend I was fine even when I was overstimulated.

At the time, I thought this was what everyone did—adjusting, blending in, trying to be easy to be around. But over the years, it became exhausting. Masking took so much mental energy that I didn't realize how tired I was until I started living in my campervan. Having that space to be alone, without constant social pressure or expectations, made me see how much effort it took to appear fine all those years.

It's only now that I'm beginning to unmask—allowing myself to show genuine reactions, admit when I'm overwhelmed, and accept that my way of processing the world isn't wrong, just different. Unmasking hasn't been easy, but it's brought a quiet relief. It feels like I'm finally meeting myself without pretending.

On Money

Some people get anxious, stressed, or even depressed because of money. But for me, I can't recall any event, situation, or stage in my life that ever led me to feel that way. Even though I was born and raised in a third-world country and understand how important money is, it has never factored into my goals, ambitions, or plans.

Of course, there were moments in my journey—while learning to improve my skills, cultivating my passions—when money was necessary to support growth, but it was never the driving force. My siblings, ex-partner, and close friends all know this, and I'm sure some of them worry about my future because of it. Still, every path I've taken has never prompted me to think about money that way.

When I was an artist, my goal was simply to be good at the craft. When I became a Pilates instructor, it was the same. And now, as a writer, my goal is to share my knowledge and my story—none of which has ever been about money.

I think my mind has created a kind of void, a barrier that separates my passions from the idea of money. Maybe that's why I feel anxious when people ask how much I charge; it's a question that touches something in me in a completely different way. Whether they pay me less or more doesn't really make a difference. Having a lot of money doesn't improve my talent or skills. My efforts in building these abilities are personal—I earned them through experience, through time, through conscious effort.

Sometimes I wish this physical piece of paper we call money could somehow infiltrate my consciousness and scrape away my ASD and anxiety. But it's far from possible, and maybe if it were, that would be the only time I'd truly see the importance of money.

> "Yet beyond this abstract reasoning, I still enjoyed observing and appreciating the things people made, bought, and experienced. I loved how these creations make society diverse yet connected, keeping everything around us interesting, vibrant, and full of life."

Final Reflections

I'm now approaching the last part of my creative journey, and I realise how interesting my life truly has been. It may seem simple on the surface—just cruising along, doing what others do, setting goals, and following through on plans. But I've come to feel that our physical existence has little to do with our conscious mind. The physical world is bound by limits, while our consciousness exists in a space without boundaries—unlimited in time and possibility. We often think it's all contained within our one-pound brain, and physically, yes, it is. But mentally, it stretches far beyond those confines. What I'm trying to say is that within our minds, we can do anything.

I'd like to think that ASD is not a disorder but rather a glimpse into what the brain might be capable of when it functions beyond what we expect. The claim that we only use one-third of our brain's capacity makes sense to me—why would we need more than that to navigate a physically limited world? Some readers or professionals in this field might say this idea leans toward insanity.

But what if those moments—when every line around me becomes more defined, when random sounds start to make sense, when a voice seems to come from nowhere, or when my mind overflows with questions—are not signs of hallucination, insanity, or even ASD, but rather moments when the brain is trying to project something into the physical world?

Maybe it's my consciousness reaching across that unseen boundary, trying to understand and make sense of the gap between it and the physical world.

I often hear people say that autistic individuals live in their own world. What if they truly do? Sometimes I feel that phrase carries a negative connotation, as if inhabiting a different world means something is wrong. But maybe it isn't wrong—maybe it's just not aligned with the mainstream perception of reality. Imagine a future where everyone is autistic and looking back at the past world as the one that was mistaken. How would that feel? We don't label our primitive ancestors as autistic simply because their ways of thinking were different from later generations. Just as evolution allows diversity in thought and behavior, autism might simply represent another natural variation of the human mind—not a flaw or disorder.

From this perspective, I think there is no way for my mind to make me fully aware that I have ASD, just as no one is ever explicitly told by their own consciousness that they are "normal." I feel that nobody can understand consciousness better than consciousness itself. When our brain evolves, our consciousness never reveals its reasoning or its plans. What we see in the outside world is only the result: we change over time. We are made observers of ourselves, left to figure it out on our own.

That's why I mentioned earlier that our physical life has little to do with our consciousness. When you think about it, whether we evolve from an amoeba to a fish, monkey, Neanderthal, or Homo sapiens, the brain doesn't care about the species it inhabits. What it cares about is continuing to evolve, achieving whatever goal it has, regardless of the form it takes.

I want to clarify again that I'm not here to make any scientific claims or propose fringe theories. I'm here to share my perspective—how I live, think, reason, and navigate myself through life. It has been interesting seeing my life in pages and being vulnerable. But it has also been a creative journey that challenged me to think deeply and stay focused throughout the process of writing this book, even with my tendency to forget certain things—the kind that feels selective, as if my mind chooses what to keep and what to let go.

Through this effort, I hope to contribute to a deeper understanding of ASD, particularly by understanding myself as well. After being diagnosed, everything began to make sense—my story, my experiences, and the way I see the world. It helps me connect my past to my present and navigate my future with more meaning and confidence. Since I've been given the chance to see both worlds and choose which path to follow, I choose to stay in the present—in the now.

www.ingramcontent.com/pod-product-compliance
Lightning Source LLC
Chambersburg PA
CBHW040043100526
44584CB00033BA/4233